The Dictionary of
Interpersonal Relationships

by

Rosemary K. West

The Dictionary of Interpersonal Relationships
Dark Cat Books, Los Angeles

ISBN-13: 978-1533599339
ISBN-10: 1533599335

To Steve, with love

Abbreviations

abbr.	abbreviation
adj.	adjective
adv.	adverb
anth.	anthropology
biol.	biology
coll.	colloquial
e.g.	for example
et al.	and others
fem.	feminine
inf.	informal
ling.	linguistics
masc.	masculine
n.	noun
obs.	obsolete
pl.	plural
psych.	psychology
soc.	sociology
U.S.	United States
v.	verb

Where there are differences in spelling, definition, or usage between British and American English, the American version has been used, unless otherwise noted.

A

abandon, *v.* 1. leave and never return to someone or something. 2. leave someone in an insecure or dangerous situation. 3. give up, discontinue, or withdraw from something.

absence makes the heart grow fonder, *proverb*. People who are apart miss each other and feel increased affection.

absolute divorce. See DIVORCE.

abuse, *v.* 1. treat someone or something in a harmful, damaging, or offensive way. 2. assault someone physically or sexually. 3. speak insultingly and cruelly. *n.* 4. bad, improper, or harmful treatment. 5. physical or sexual assault. 6. harsh, insulting, or degrading language.

accommodate, *v.* 1. be helpful or do someone a favor. 2. adapt or make a suitable adjustment. 3. provide food, lodging, or space.

accomplice, *n.* a person who helps another commit a crime or get into mischief.

accountability partner, someone who acts as a coach or counselor for the purpose of helping another keep a commitment.

acquaintance, *n.* 1. a person one knows, usually not a close friend. 2. the state of being acquainted or knowing someone.

active listening, *psych.* a technique of mindful listening and responding intended to improve understanding.

adelphic polyandry. See FRATERNAL POLYANDRY.

adopt, *v.* 1. take a child as one's own, especially through a formal legal process. 2. take permanent custody of a pet which has been previously lost or abandoned.

adoption, *n.* the act or process of adopting a child. A legally adopted child has all the same legal, moral, and familial relationships, rights, privileges, and obligations as a child born into the family.

adoptive, *adj*. 1. having to do with adoption. 2. related by adoption.

adulation, *n*. excessive admiration.

adult, *n*. 1. someone who has reached full physical maturity. 2. someone who has reached the legal age of majority, or the age of consent.

adult child, 1. one's child who has reached adulthood. Also called a **grown child**. 2. an adult whose behavior is consistently immature and selfish. 3. **adult child of alcoholics**, someone who has experienced adverse emotional or psychological effects as the result of having one or more alcoholic parents.

adultery, *n*. a sexual relationship between a married person and someone who is not that person's spouse. Adultery is also referred to as **infidelity** or **cheating**.
      Adultery has been decriminalized in most industrialized nations as well as many other countries throughout the world. It is still illegal in a few U.S. states, although the laws are rarely enforced. In some of the countries where adultery is still illegal, penalties are severe, and may include capital punishment.

adversary, *n*. 1. an enemy; a person or group that opposes or attacks another. 2. an opponent in a contest or sporting event.

adviser, **advisor**, *n*. 1. someone who gives advice. 2. a teacher or school official who helps students select classes.

advocate, *n*. 1. someone who speaks or writes in support of another. 2. someone who pleads a case in court. 3. someone who supports a cause or a course of action. *v*. 4. argue in favor of or publicly support a cause or course of action.

affair, *n*. 1. anything that needs to be done, (e.g. business affairs). 2. a matter of interest, concern, or duty. 3. an illicit romantic or sexual relationship, particularly if one or both of the parties are married to someone else. An **emotional affair** is an affair that has not been consummated, or one in which the emphasis is on the emotional connection between the affair partners.

affection, *n*. fondness; kind or loving feelings.

affianced, *adj*. *archaic*. engaged to be married.

affinity, *n*. 1. a natural liking or attraction for a person or thing. 2. a relationship by marriage or other non-genetic connection. 3. a kinship relationship that exists when one person is related by blood to another person's spouse. A formula for calculating degrees of affinity is used in legal contexts.

affirmation, *n*. 1. a declaration that something is true. 2. an indication of agreement. 3. a positive statement intended to provide encouragement.

affirmative consent, the requirement that both parties overtly agree in order to establish that sexual activity is consensual.

affront, *n*. an offensive or outrageous remark or action.

agamy, *n*. *anth*. 1. absence of marriage regulations within a society. 2. absence or nonrecognition of marriage.

agápē, agape, *n*. *Ancient Greek*. The highest form of universal love; love of humanity; love shared between God and humankind. In ancient times the word was also used to indicate love for spouse and family.

age-gap relationship. See MAY-DECEMBER ROMANCE.

agent, *n*. someone who is authorized to act on behalf of another.

age of consent, the age at which a person is legally considered able to consent to marriage or sexual relations. The age of consent varies from place to place. In the U.S. it differs from state to state, falling between 16 and 18, and some states permit marriage at a younger age with parental consent or in the case of pregnancy. In some countries the age of consent is as low as 12. A few countries do not specify an age limit for consent, but may have other restrictions, such as outlawing any sexual relations outside of marriage regardless of age.

aggregate, *n*. *soc*. a number of people in the same place at the same time.

aggression, *n*. an attack or hostile action in any form, whether physical, verbal, or symbolic.

aggressive, *adj*. 1. displaying hostility or performing acts of aggression. 2. highly forceful and bold.

agree to disagree, *idiom.* remain cordial while holding different opinions.

aide, *n.* an official assistant.

aide-de-camp, *n.* a military officer who acts as an official, confidential assistant to a superior officer.

alexithymia, *n. psych.* a condition in which individuals have difficulty experiencing, identifying, understanding, and describing emotions.

alienate, *v.* 1. cause someone to feel indifferent or hostile. 2. cause someone to be withdrawn or isolated.

alienation of affection, *law.* estrangement of spouses caused by a third party's intentional interference. In a few states, this may be grounds for a lawsuit.

alienist, *n. archaic.* a psychiatrist or psychologist, especially one who evaluates mental competency for legal purposes.

alimony, *n.* the legal obligation of one spouse to provide financial support for the other during a separation or following a divorce. Also called **spousal support** or **spousal maintenance**.

allegiance, *n.* loyalty.

alliance, *n.* 1. the merging of efforts or interests by individuals or groups 2. a group of people who have joined together for common interests.

ally, *n.* a person or group that is united with another in the support of common interests.

alone, *adj.* 1. solitary; without the presence of others. 2. exclusive or unique: "She is alone in her ability to excel."

alpha male, 1. in zoology, a male animal that is the leader of a group or pack; a male animal that is dominant over other males. 2. *idiom.* a man who has strong leadership qualities and exerts authority in business and social situations.

altercation, *n.* a noisy, angry dispute.

alter ego, *Latin*, meaning "another I." 1. a person who can act as a perfect substitute for someone. 2. a very intimate or inseparable friend who shares many similarities with oneself.

altruism, *n*. unselfish or self-sacrificing concern and care for others. **Kin altruism** (sometimes called **nepotistic altruism**) is altruistic behavior toward one's relatives. **Reciprocal altruism** is altruism that has a selfish component, in that it is given with the expectation of eventual reciprocity.

amanuensis, *n. obs.* a person employed as a secretary or transcriptionist.

amatory, *adj.* pertaining to love.

amigo (*masc.*), **amiga** (*fem.*), *n. Spanish.* friend.

analysand, *n. psych.* a person undergoing psychoanalysis.

ancestor, *n.* one from whom a person is descended; a forefather or foremother.

ancestry, *n.* 1. one's lineage, descent, or genetic background. 2. a series of ancestors.

androphobia, *n.* fear of men.

anima, *n.* 1. one's inner self or soul. 2. in Jungian psychology, an inner feminine quality of the male personality.

animosity, *n.* a feeling of ill will or enmity.

animus, *n.* 1. hostility. 2. motivation to act. 3. in Jungian psychology, an inner masculine quality of the female personality.

anniversary, *n.* the yearly recurrence or celebration of a date or event. The word is derived from the Latin word for year, and technically refers only to yearly events. However, people often apply it to smaller increments, such as a one-month or six-month anniversary of an occasion.

annulment, *n.* a procedure that cancels a marriage. Unlike divorce, which simply terminates the marriage, annulment treats the marriage as if it did not exist. Annulments are granted when the marriage was illegal or invalid, as in cases of fraud or bigamy, one party being underage, or when the marriage is not consummated. Some people seek a religious annulment even when they do not qualify for a legal one.

antagonist, *n*. an enemy or opponent.

antagonize, *v*. make someone .angry

antisocial, *adj*. 1. preferring to avoid the company of others. 2. unable or unwilling to socialize with others. 3. contrary to or antagonistic toward the norms of society.

antisocial personality disorder, *psych*. a mental health disorder characterized by lack of empathy, extreme disregard for others. arrogance, and illegal behavior.

apologize, *v*. express regret or remorse for having wronged or failed another.

apology, *n*. the expression or act of apologizing .

appease, *v*. 1. pacify or soothe someone, especially by giving in to demands. 2. relieve or satisfy a feeling: "The ice cream appeased his hunger."

apple doesn't fall far from the tree, the, *proverb*. Children tend to be like their parents.

apple of [someone]'s eye, *idiom*. one who is highly favored by some-one. Historically, the pupil of the eye was referred to as the apple. The pupil is very precious, and thus refers to someone especially precious.

apprentice, *n*. 1. a person who works for another in order to learn a trade. 2. someone who is new at the job and is still learning.

apprenticeship, *n*. 1. the job or condition of an apprentice. 2. the period during which one is an apprentice.

archenemy, *n*. 1. a major enemy. 2. the Devil.

argue, *v*. 1. present reasons for or against something. 2. engage in a dispute with someone.

argument, *n*. 1. a discussion or debate regarding different points of view. 2. a disagreement or dispute. 3. a statement of fact or opinion for or against something. 4. the theme or main point of a paper or speech.

arranged marriage, a marriage that is planned and agreed to by the families, guardians, or representatives of the bride and groom.

Arranged marriage is common in many countries, particularly those where cultural traditions or laws prohibit or restrict socializing between the sexes. Typically, once a match is found, the prospective spouses are introduced. In some cases they meet only briefly, in others they have a brief courtship period to become better acquainted. Ideally, the marriage takes place only if the couple consents. However, in many cases the couple may have little or no choice. See CHILD MARRIAGE, FORCED MARRIAGE.

asexual, *adj.* 1. being neither male nor female. 2. having no sexual interest or response. 3. unrelated to sexual processes.

ask [someone] out, invite someone to go on a date.

assassinate. See HOMICIDE.

assault, *n.* or *v.* attack.

assertiveness training, a type of behavior therapy intended to help individuals learn to appropriately and effectively express their opinions, needs, and desires.

assistance animal. See SERVICE ANIMAL.

associate, *n.* 1. a colleague or fellow worker; someone who is connected to another through work or business 2. a friend, companion, or acquaintance. 3. someone with limited membership in an organization. 4. a person or organization that is connected to or cooperates with a particular organization. *v.* 5. mentally connect or see a relationship between two things. 6. connect oneself with an organization, activity, or idea. 7. come into contact with someone through social or business activities.

at loggerheads, *idiom.* in a state of intense disagreement.

at odds, *idiom.* in conflict; unable to agree.

attachment, *n.* a feeling that connects someone to a person, place, thing, or idea; an emotional connection.

attachment style, *psych.* a description of the emotional and behavioral pattern with which one connects to significant others. See ATTACHMENT THEORY.

attachment theory, *psych*. a concept that describes and explains the need to form a close, stable emotional bond with another person, starting with the infant's relationship with a primary caregiver. Attachment theory was introduced by British psychoanalyst John Bowlby (1907 - 1990), and further researched and developed by psychologist Mary Ainsworth (1913 - 1999).

audience, *n*. 1. a group of spectators or listeners at a performance or event. 2. the people who are reached by a book, television program, blog, advertisement, etc. 3. followers or fans. 4. a formal meeting with a prominent person.

audience effect, *psych*. the impact that the presence of passive observers has on one's performance of a task.

aunt, *n*. 1. the sister of one's father or mother. 2. the wife of one's uncle. 3. an honorary title sometimes used by children for adult women who are family friends.

authority, *n*. 1. the right or power to command, control, decide, or enforce. 2. someone who is an expert on a topic. 3. an accepted source of valid information.

authorize, *v*. grant someone the power or right to do something.

avatar, *n*. 1. in Hinduism, the incarnation of a god. 2. an image or symbol representing a person online.

avoidance relationship, *anth*. in some cultures, a family relationship between persons who are, by tradition, forbidden to have physical or verbal contact with each other.

avoidant personality disorder, *psych*. an emotional disorder characterized by feelings of inadequacy, hypersensitivity to criticism, and social inhibition.

avuncular, *adj*. characteristic of an uncle; acting like an uncle.

avunculate marriage, marriage between an uncle and niece or aunt and nephew. See INCEST.

B

baby, *n*. 1. a young child, from birth to three or four years old. A **newborn** is a baby less than a month old. **Neonate** is a medical term for a newborn. **Infant** usually means a baby less than a year old. A **toddler** is a baby just learning to walk. 2. an endearment. 3. *coll*. one's sweetheart. *v*. 4. treat someone with special care, like a baby.

baby daddy, *slang*. a man who fathered a child as the result of an affair or casual relationship. The term is generally considered demeaning.

baby mama, *slang*. a mother whose child was fathered by someone with whom she did not have a committed relationship. The term is generally considered demeaning.

baby minder, *British*. babysitter.

baby of the family, *idiom*. the youngest (typically the last) child in a family, often treated with special favor.

babysitter, *n*. someone who watches over children in the absence of their parents.

baby talk, 1. the speech of young children just learning to talk. 2. a simplified, stylized way of speaking used by caretakers toward young children, sometimes called **motherese**.

bachelor, *n*. an unmarried man. A **confirmed bachelor** is a man who is (or seems) firmly committed to remaining single. In the past, "confirmed bachelor" was sometimes used as a euphemism for a homosexual man. An **eligible bachelor** is an unmarried man who is considered desirable as a possible husband.

bachelorette. *n*. an unmarried young woman.

bachelorette party, a party given by a woman's friends when she is about to be married.

bachelor party, a party given by a man's friends when he is about to married.

backbite, *v*. speak maliciously about someone who is not present.

back-channeling, *n. ling*. In conversation, indications that the listener is paying attention and understands the speaker, typically interjections such as "I see" or "uh-huh," or small gestures such as a nod.

backhanded compliment, *idiom*. an insult disguised as a compliment.

back-seat driver, *idiom*. 1. a passenger in a car who persists in instructing the driver. Originated in the 1920s. 2. a person who is not in charge but tries to give instructions.

back talk, rude or defiant remarks made to a person in authority.

bad blood, *idiom*. ill will; unfriendly relations.

baggage, *idiom*. in the context of one's personality or emotional makeup: ideas, thought patterns, or emotional burdens from the past that interfere with one's ability to function well in life, particularly in personal relationships.

ball and chain, *idiom*. a derogatory expression for one's spouse. The imagery comes from the iron ball and chain sometimes attached to prisoners' ankles to keep them from escaping.

bandwagon. See jump on the bandwagon.

banns, *n*. a traditional notice of an intended marriage, announced or posted at the church of the engaged couple, or at the local courthouse.

banter. *n*. a friendly exchange of playful, teasing remarks.

baseball widow. See SPORTS WIDOW.

bastard, *n*. 1. *archaic*. someone born to unmarried parents. 2. *slang*. a vicious, disliked person.

battered woman/man/child/person, a victim of domestic violence; someone who has been physically abused.

battered woman syndrome, *psych*. a psychological disorder arising in situations of domestic violence, in which the victim develops a number of emotional and psychological problems, and feels helpless to leave the relationship. Sometimes used as part of a self-defense plea when a domestic abuse victim is accused of murdering the abuser. Also called battered wife syndrome, battered spouse syndrome, and battered person syndrome.

beard, *n. slang.* someone who is presented as a person's companion or escort in order to conceal the identity of the person's actual partner.

bear hug, a hearty, tight hug.

bear ill will, have angry feelings toward someone; hold a grudge.

beau, *pl.* beaus, beaux. *n.* 1. an attentive male companion. 2. a boyfriend or admirer.

Beauty and the Beast, a French fairy tale in which a beautiful young woman is required to live with an ugly beast. Eventually her love breaks the spell that had transformed him from a prince into a beast. With his true form restored, they are married. Often mentioned in reference to a seemingly mismatched couple. The theme of a bewitched or disguised prince appears in many stories. See KISS A FROG.

become an item, *idiom.* become a romantically involved couple.

bedfellow, *n.* someone who shares a bed.

beget, *v.* procreate.

begrudge, *v.* 1. be resentful or reluctant to give or allow. 2. be resentful or disapproving of another's good fortune.

belittle, *v.* portray or speak of someone or something as less important or effective than it appears to be.

beloved, *adj.* 1. loved. *n.* 2. a person who is loved.

benefactor, *n.* someone who kindly provides assistance, especially financial assistance, to individuals or groups.

besotted, *adj.* infatuated.

best friend, one's closest or favorite friend.

best man. See GROOMSMAN.

besty, **bestie**, *n. coll.* a shortened form of BEST FRIEND.

betroth, *v.* arrange for a couple to be married.

betrothal, *n.* 1. the act of becoming betrothed. 2. the period of time during which one is betrothed.

betrothed, *adj.* 1. engaged to be married. *n.* 2. the person to whom one is engaged.

betray, *v.* 1. harm someone through treachery or disloyalty. 2. break a trust or violate a confidence. 3. unconsciously or unintentionally reveal something one would prefer to hide.

better half, *idiom.* one's spouse.

BFF, *abbr.* best friend forever.

bicker, *v.* argue about petty matters.

bigamy, *n.* illegally entering into a marriage contract while still legally married to a prior spouse. This is a crime in countries whose only legally recognized form of marriage is monogamy. A person who commits bigamy is a **bigamist**. See POLYGAMY.
     The difference between bigamy and polygamy is both legal and social. In societies where polygamy is legal, bigamy is not a problem. In societies where polygamy is illegal, polygamists are usually prosecuted under bigamy laws. Bigamy is typically secretive, with each of the bigamist's spouses being unaware of the others. Polygamy is typically open, with all spouses being aware of each other, whether or not they live together.

big fish in a small pond, *idiom.* someone who is important or powerful, but only within a very small group.

biodad *n. coll.* birth father.

biological parent, the genetic parent of a child.

biomom *n. coll.* birth mother.

birds of a feather flock together, *proverb.* People with similar characteristics and interests like to spend time with each other.

birth father, the biological father of a child. This term is often used when a child has been adopted, to differentiate the biological father from the adoptive father. It is also sometimes used when the biological father is estranged from the child.

birth mother, a woman who gives birth to a child. This term is often used when a child has been adopted, to differentiate the biological mother from the adoptive mother. It is also sometimes used when the biological mother is estranged from the child. In some cases the birth mother may be not be the child's biological mother, as when a donor egg has been used. See SURROGATE MOTHER.

birth order, the sequence in which children are born into a family. Often believed to have a significant influence on one's personality.

bisexual, *adj.* sexually attracted to both men and women.

bite the hand that feeds you, *idiom.* betray or show hostility toward someone who has treated one kindly, or who provides one with support.

blackball, *v.* exclude someone from a group. Derived from the practice of private clubs that voted on the admission of a new member by having current members drop black or white balls into a box. A single black ball would cause admission to be denied.

blackmail, *n.* 1. a scheme in which payment is extorted by threats, particularly the threat of exposing the victim's secrets, or of causing injury to loved ones. 2. **emotional blackmail**, controlling someone with whom one has a relationship by using guilt and fear, withholding approval, threatening to end the relationship, etc.

black sheep, *idiom.* a person who is considered a disgrace to a family or group.

black widow, *idiom.* a woman who kills one or more husbands or boyfriends, especially for material gain. Derived from the behavior of the black widow spider, which occasionally eats the male after mating.

blame, *v.* 1. assign responsibility for a problem, error, or wrongdoing. 2. censure or find fault with someone. *n.* 3. responsibility for anything deserving of censure. 4. To **take the blame** is to admit responsibility or guilt.

blended family. See FAMILY.

blind date, 1. a date or social engagement with a person one has not previously met. 2. one of the people participating in such a date.

blood, *n.* when used in reference to families: 1. descent from a common ancestor. 2. close family relationships. 3. a closely related person.

blood brother, 1. a male friend who has sworn loyalty, often involving a ceremony in which two men cut themselves and mingle the blood. 2. a brother related by birth.

blood is thicker than water, *proverb.* Family ties are stronger than other relationships.

bloodline, *n.* a line of descent; a pedigree.

blood relatives, people who are genetically related to each other; people related by birth.

Bluebeard, *n.* 1. the main character in a French folktale. He murdered several wives and kept their bodies in a locked room. 2. any man believed to have murdered a number of wives or girlfriends.

bluff, *v.* 1. attempt to mislead others by appearing bold or confident. *n.* 2. an instance of bluffing.
      To **call [someone]'s bluff** is to challenge or expose someone who appears to be bluffing.

body language, nonverbal communication through gestures, movements, posture, etc., whether intentional or unintentional.

bond, *n.* 1. a connection based on an agreement or obligation. 2. a connection based on common interests or similar characteristics. 3. an emotional connection or friendship. *v.* 4. form a connection.

Bonnie and Clyde, Bonnie Parker (1910-1934) and Clyde Barrow (1909-1934), a couple who went on a violent crime spree in the 1930s until they were killed by police. Sometimes used to refer to an obsessively involved couple, especially a couple involved in crime or mischief.

bosom buddy, bosom friend, a very close friend and confidant.

boss, *n.* 1. an employer or someone who supervises workers. 2. someone who controls a political party. 3. someone in a position of authority.

boyfriend, *n.* a male companion, usually in the context of dating or romance.

brawl, *n*. a loud or rough argument or fight.

breach of promise, *law*. violation of a promise to marry someone. In some states this may be grounds for a lawsuit.

breadwinner, *n*. a person who earns income that provides support for a family.

break [someone]'s heart, cause someone tremendous disappointment and grief.

break the ice, *idiom*. relieve tension between people meeting for the first time; facilitate conversation among new acquaintances.

break up 1. end a relationship. 2. interrupt an activity, especially by separating the participants.

breakup, *n*. the process of ending a relationship.

bride, *n*. a newly married woman or a woman about to be married.

bridegroom, *n*. a newly married man or a man about to be married. Often shortened to "groom".

bridesmaid, *n*. a woman who serves as a ceremonial attendant to the bride at her wedding. The chief attendant is the **maid of honor** (if single) or **matron of honor** (if married or widowed).

bride price, money or property paid by the groom or his family to the family of the bride. See DOWRY.

bring up a child, take care of a child during the formative years, especially in regard to teaching proper behavior and values.

bro, *n*. *slang*. a close male friend. Short for "brother".

broadwife, *n*. *obs*. in U.S. history, a female slave whose husband was owned by a different master.

broken heart, a state of extreme grief or sorrow, especially over the loss of a close relationship.

broken home, *idiom*. a family in which one of the parents has moved out; a family disrupted by divorce.

broken up, *idiom*. 1. emotionally distraught. 2. in the state of having ended a relationship.

bromance, *slang*. a very close, nonsexual relationship between two men. Coined in the mid 2000s by combining "brother" and "romance".

brother, *n*. 1. a male sibling. 2. a very close male friend, treated like a brother. 3. a monk or member of a religious order. 4. a male member of the same church. 5. a fellow member of an association, such as a fraternity. 6. a fellow human being regarded with a sense of kindness or equality.

brotherhood, *n*. 1. the state of being a brother; the relationship between brothers. 2. fellowship; close friendship. 3. a fraternal or trade organization. 4. people engaged in the same profession who share common interests. 5. a sense of equality and kindness extended to all people.

brother-in-law, *pl*. brothers-in-law. *n*. the husband of one's sister or the brother of one's wife.

brothers in arms, soldiers who serve together, especially in combat.

brother's keeper, *idiom*. A person who is responsible for someone else. From the Bible story in which Cain kills his brother Abel and then disclaims responsibility by asking, "Am I my brother's keeper?"

buddy, *n*. 1. a comrade or chum. 2. a form of address to a child or pet, especially one whose name is unknown. 3. a form of address to a man whose name is not known, sometimes considered demeaning.

bully, *n*. 1. an aggressive, domineering person who habitually browbeats and intimidates others, especially if they are smaller and weaker. *v*. 2. dominate, intimidate, and harass others.

bump into [someone], *idiom*. encounter someone unexpectedly.

bundling, *n*. a courtship practice of 18th century America. A young man and woman were placed together in bed, fully clothed, sometimes wrapped in separate blankets, and often separated by a barrier known as a **bundling board**. They were expected to converse and to avoid sexual contact.

bunkmate, *n*. someone who shares sleeping quarters; one who sleeps in a nearby bunk or bed.

bury the hatchet, *idiom.* make peace between individuals or groups. Derived from a Native American practice of burying weapons as a symbolic gesture.

buss, *n.* or *v. archaic.* kiss.

busybody, *n.* someone who pries into or meddles in the affairs of others.

butler, *n.* the chief manservant in a household.

butter [someone] up, *idiom.* flatter someone in order to gain favor.

buttinsky, *n. slang.* someone who interrupts or interferes in others' conversations and activities.

butt of the joke, *idiom.* a person who is targeted for ridicule, especially as part of an anecdote or joke.

bystander, *n.* a person who is present but uninvolved.

bystander effect, *psych.* the phenomenon in which people are less likely to help someone in an emergency if others are present.

cabal, *n.* a small group of conspirators, especially one that exists secretly within an organization or government.

cahoots, *inf.* a partnership, especially one involving a conspiracy or secret.

camaraderie, *n.* comradeship.

captive, *n.* 1. a prisoner or hostage. 2. someone who is psychologically enslaved.

care, *v.* 1. feel concern or interest. 2. like or have a special preference for. 3. be attentive to someone's needs: "He cared for the sick child." 4. have a desire or inclination: "Would you care for dessert?" 5. **take care**, be cautious. 6. **take care of [someone]**, provide for someone's needs; watch over someone. 7. **take care of [something]**, make sure that an action is performed or that a problem is solved. *n.* 8. caution and effort exerted to do something safely or correctly: "He used great care in repairing the bridge." 9. actions performed to keep someone safe and healthy: "We need to provide better care for the elderly." 10. protection: "The baby was left in the care of its grandparents."

caregiver, *n.* someone who provides for the needs of a child or a sick, disabled, or elderly person.

caretaker, *n.* 1. caregiver. 2. someone who is in charge of the maintenance of land or other property in the owner's absence. 3. someone who takes care of animals.

carnal knowledge, *idiom.* sexual intercourse.

carry the torch for [someone], *idiom.* have ongoing romantic feelings for someone who does not feel the same way or who is unavailable.

Casanova, *n.* a man who habitually seduces many women. After Giovanni Jacopo Casanova (1728-95), an Italian adventurer and writer.

caste, *n.* 1. in Hindu culture, a hereditary social group with strict rules and limitations that distinguish it from other such groups. 2. a highly rigid system of social distinctions. 3. a distinct social class or group sharing common cultural features.

castigate, *v.* severely criticize or punish.

casual acquaintance, a person one knows slightly.

casual sex, sexual interactions with strangers or slight acquaintances; brief sexual relationships.

catch [someone]'s eye, *idiom.* attract someone's attention.

celibacy, *n.* abstention from marriage or sexual relations. Celibacy often refers to vows taken by members of religious orders who remain unmarried.

celibate, *n.* 1. a person who abstains from marriage and sexual relations. *adj.* 2. not engaging in sexual relations.

cellmate, *n.* a person who shares the same cell in jail.

champion, *n.* 1. someone who holds first place in a competition after defeating an opponent or series of opponents. 2. someone who defends or fights for a person, group, or cause. *v.* 3. defend or support.

chaperone, chaperon, *n.* 1. a person who accompanies and supervises minors at an event or on a trip. 2. an adult who accompanies a child in public in order to ensure safety and good behavior. 3. anyone who has the responsibility of accompanying and looking after individuals or groups in circumstances where proper behavior or safety is a concern. *v.* 4. act as a chaperone.

charge, *n.* in reference to a person: someone placed in one's care.

charisma, *n.* 1. an attractive personal quality of great charm and appeal. 2. a particularly magnetic personality in a leader, inspiring great enthusiasm and loyalty.

charm, *n.* 1. the ability to please and attract people through personality and manner. *v.* 2. attract and please someone through appearance or manner. 3. affect someone as if by a magic spell.

charming, *adj.* pleasing; delightful.

chaste, *adj.* virtuous and decent, especially regarding sexual matters.

chat, *n*. 1. an informal conversation. *v*. 2. engage in an informal conversation. 3. have a real-time online conversation with someone.

chat [someone] up, talk to someone in an informal, friendly way, especially with a purpose, such as flattery or getting information.

cheat, *v*. 1. defraud or swindle someone. 2. practice deceit. 3. violate rules and regulations. 4. be unfaithful in a monogamous relationship (often phrased as "cheating on" someone). *n*. 5. a person who cheats. 6. an act or method of cheating.

chemistry, *n*. *coll*. an affinity or attraction between two people; rapport.

child, *pl*. children. *n*. 1. someone who has not yet reached physical maturity. 2. someone who is below the age of legal adulthood or the age of consent; a minor. 3. a son or daughter.

child abuse, any kind of maltreatment, abusive actions, neglect, or molestation perpetrated against a child, especially when done by a parent or other caretaker.

childbirth, *n*. the process of giving birth to a child, from the beginning of labor, as the infant moves from the womb through the birth canal, to the moment of delivery to the outside world.

child bride, 1. a woman who married at a very young age. 2. a girl entering into a child marriage.

child custody, the legal right, granted by a court, to control the care, maintenance, living arrangements, and other matters regarding one's child.

child marriage, a marriage in which one or both spouses are children. Although child marriage is widely considered a human rights violation and is illegal in most countries, forced marriage between young girls and older men is still common in many parts of the world. See AGE OF CONSENT, FORCED MARRIAGE.

child support, court ordered payments, typically made by a non-custodial parent, to support one's minor children. Child support is usually ordered as part of a divorce or legal separation, or as the result of a paternity suit.

chip off the old block, *idiom.* someone who has characteristics strongly resembling those of his or her parent.

chum, *n.* a close friend or companion.

chummy, *adj.* very friendly.

circle, *n.* when used in reference to groups of people: 1. a small group of people connected by a shared interest or activity, such as a **sewing circle.** 2. **family circle,** a closely related group of people, especially those who live together or who are in frequent contact with each other. 3. **social circle,** a group of people who are all acquainted with each other. 4. **circle of influence,** a geographical area or a social network in which one exerts power.

civil ceremony. See WEDDING.

civil union, a legally recognized union of a same-sex couple, with rights similar to those of marriage.

clan, *n.* 1. a group of families or households who are, or who consider themselves, descended from a common ancestor. 2. a large family or group believed to be of common descent. 3. a large extended family.

clannish, *adj.* preferring to associate with one's own group to the exclusion of outsiders.

clansman, clanswoman, *n.* a member of a clan.

classmate, *n.* a member of the same class at school.

clear the air, *idiom.* correct a misunderstanding or resolve a disagreement.

click, *v. idiom.* have personalities that fit together; easily function well together.

client, *n.* a customer, especially of a professional, such as an attorney, or of a social or government agency.

climb on the bandwagon. See JUMP ON THE BANDWAGON.

clingy, *adj.* in reference to people: 1. tending to cling or hold on, such as a young child always grasping and reaching for a parent. 2. anxiously attempting to stay near or in be in very frequent contact with someone.

clique, *n.* a small group of friends or associates who exclude others.

clone, *n.* an organism that is an exact genetic copy of another. Identical twins are naturally-occurring clones.

close-knit, *adj.* bound or united by strong relationships or family ties.

club, *n.* a group of people organized for some common purpose.

co-, prefix meaning joint, with, accompanying, or together: co-conspirator, cohabit, cooperative, co-pilot, coworker.

coach, *n.* 1. a person who trains athletes. 2. a private trainer or tutor. 3. someone who provides advice and encouragement. *v.* 4. provide training to athletes. 5. act as a private trainer or tutor. 6. provide advice and encouragement.

coaction effect, *psych.* the effect on one's performance of a task when others are present and engaged in the same task.

coddle, *v.* treat someone very indulgently or in an over-protective way.

codependency, *n.* a dysfunctional relationship in which one partner supports and enables the other's addiction, mental illness, or other destructive and unhealthy behavior.

cognate, *adj.* 1. related by birth. *n.* 2. a person who is related to one by birth.

cohabit, *v.* live together as if married.

cohabitation, *n.* the practice of living together for an extended period of time as if married. When a couple lives together for the purpose of determining compatibility prior to marriage, cohabitation is sometimes referred to as **trial marriage**.

cohesive, *adj.* in reference to people: having a close, harmonious relationship; united.

cohort, *n.* 1. historically, a division of a Roman legion. 2. a group of people connected by a common interest or purpose. 3. a group of people connected by a particular characteristic, such as age. 4. a companion or classmate.

coitus, *n.* sexual intercourse.

cold shoulder, the, *idiom*. obvious indifference or unfriendly treatment.

collaborate, *v*. 1. work together on a project. 2. help the enemy of one's country.

colleague, *n*. an associate in an office, workplace, or profession.

collective wedding, a wedding ceremony in which many different couples are married at the same time. Also called a **mass wedding** or **group wedding**.

collectivism, *n*. an economic theory or system in which all land and the means of production are owned and controlled by the state or by the group as a whole.

colloquy, *n*. a conversation or dialogue.

come on to [someone], *idiom*. try to attract someone romantically or sexually.

comfort animal. See THERAPY ANIMAL.

commit, *v*. 1. make a promise, pledge or vow to do something. 2. be dedicated to something. 3. pledge or dedicate resources for a particular purpose or course of action. 4. carry out a crime, misdeed, or error. 5. transfer to a place or condition of preservation. 6. send to confinement in a mental hospital. 7. entrust for safekeeping.

commitment, *n*. 1. a promise, pledge, or vow. 2. an obligation. 3. strong dedication. 4. confinement in a mental hospital.

commitment phobia, *coll*. strong anxiety or fear of staying in a long-term relationship.

committed, *adj*. dedicated to a person, group, cause, or course of action.

committed relationship, a romantic or sexual relationship which is intended to be long-term and, usually, monogamous.

committee, *n*. a group of people set up for a specific purpose.

common-law marriage, a legally recognized marriage between a couple that has not undergone a formal ceremony or registration of the marriage. Common-law marriage is now rare in the U.S., and is recognized by only a handful of states. Contrary to popular misconceptions, simply living together does not create a common-law marriage. Certain conditions must be met. These usually require that the couple be legally able to marry, that they intend to be married, that they publicly present themselves as married, and that they live together for a specified amount of time. Once properly established, a common-law marriage has all the same rights and obligations as a formal marriage, and can be terminated only by divorce or death. Nevertheless, legally proving the existence of a common-law marriage can be challenging, and it may be difficult for common-law spouses to inherit property or to receive pension payments or other benefits.

communal marriage. See GROUP MARRIAGE.

commune, *n*. 1. in France, Italy, and other countries, the smallest territorial division, governed by a mayor and administrative council. 2. a group of people living together in a community or large household, sharing property and responsibilities.

communicate, *v*. present or exchange information, thoughts, or feelings.

communication, *n*. 1. the process of communicating. 2. the information or message being communicated.

community, *n*. 1. a group of any size whose members reside in a specific area and share the same government, and who may share a common historical or cultural heritage. 2. a social group sharing common characteristics or interests that are perceived as making it distinct from the larger surrounding society. 3. a neighborhood.

community of practice, *soc*. a group of people who come together for a joint activity and who share social practices.

community property, a legal arrangement whereby the property, assets, and debts acquired by either partner during the course of a marriage are owned equally by both people.
    Typically, a spouse's separate property includes anything owned prior to the marriage, as well as inheritances or gifts received during the marriage. However, if separate property is mingled with community property, it becomes part of the community property. In the event of a divorce, all community assets and debts are divided equally between the spouses. In the event of a spouse's death, inheritance laws affecting community property vary from state to state and may depend on whether or

not there are children. Only a handful of U.S. states have community property laws, although some have laws that are similar in some respects. In case of divorce, most states have "equitable distribution" laws. A prenuptial agreement can be used to override some aspects of community property and equitable distribution laws.

compadre, *n. coll.* a good friend and companion. Derived from the Spanish word for godfather.

companion, *n.* 1. a person who accompanies another. 2. a person who is frequently in the company of one or more regular associates.

companion animal, a pet.

companionate marriage, 1. a marriage whose primary focus is on affectionate companionship. 2. *archaic.* a concept promoted by social reformers in the 1920s. In a marriage of equals, partners would agree not to have children, marrying for companionship, sexual love, and shared interests. They could divorce through mutual consent, with no subsequent financial obligation. See EGALITARIAN MARRIAGE.

company, *n.* 1. a guest or guests. 2. companionship. 3. a group of people gathered together, especially for socializing or a common purpose. 4. a business organization. 5. a division or subdivision of a military, maritime, or protective organization.

compassion, *n.* 1. a feeling of deep sympathy and concern for another. 2. a strong desire to alleviate another's pain or suffering.

compatible, *adj.* able to co-exist or perform together without conflict. The condition or feeling of being compatible is **compatibility**.

compatriot, *n.* someone from the same country.

compete, *v.* 1. try to gain something by striving against others. 2. participate in a contest.

competition, *n.* 1. the act of competing. 2. a contest. 3. a rival or competitor.

competitor, *n.* 1. an individual or group that competes against others. 2. one's adversary in a competition or rivalry.

complementarity, *n. psych.* 1. the idea that in social situations people perform behaviors that are designed to evoke particular kinds of complementary or reciprocal responses from others. 2. the theory that in social relationships people seek others who have characteristics or qualities that are missing or underdeveloped in themselves, thus creating a sense of completeness or balance and enabling them to cooperate comfortably and productively. 3. a theory used to describe relationships which are structured and limited by polar-opposite roles assumed by each person, such as active/passive. In **conjunctive complementarity**, each person tends to be accepting or comfortable with his or her role. In **disjunctive complementarity**, one or both people feel forced into an undesirable or dissatisfying role.

compliment, *n.* 1. an expression of praise or admiration. 2. *idiom.* **give [someone] my compliments**, give someone greetings or good wishes on my behalf. *v.* 3. praise someone. 4. To **pay a compliment** is to express praise to someone. 5. *idiom.* To **pay one's compliments** to someone is to offer a courteous greeting.

complot, *rare.* *v.* 1. conspire together. *n.* 2. a conspiracy.

compromise, *n.* 1. an agreement or settlement reached when all parties make concessions. 2. middle ground between two ideas or things. *v.* 3. reach an agreement or settlement by making concessions. 4. endanger or affect unfavorably.

computer-mediated communication, any method of communication using computers or similar devices. Examples include email, social networking, and texting.

comrade, *n.* 1. a companion, associate, or friend. 2. a fellow member of an organization. 3. a member of the Communist party.

comrade in arms, a fellow soldier.

con, con game, confidence game, any form of fraud that uses the victim's confidence in the fraudster in order to trick the victim out of money or property. To defraud people in this way is to **con** them. A person who perpetrates this kind of fraud is known as a **confidence man, con artist, con man,** or **con woman.** (Note that as a noun, "con" is sometimes a shortened form of "convict".)

conciliate, *v.* 1. placate, appease, or overcome distrust. 2. reconcile.

concubine, *n.* 1. in polygamous societies, a woman who cohabits with a man but has a lower status than a wife. 2. *obs.* a married man's mistress.

condescend, *v.* 1. behave as if one is descending from a superior position in order to accommodate an inferior. 2. haughtily perform an action as if it is of little importance.

conduct disorder, *psych.* an emotional disorder, diagnosed in childhood or adolescence, characterized by a pattern of antisocial behavior.

confederate, *n.* 1. an ally. 2. an accomplice.

confessor, *n.* a priest or other clergyperson to whom one confesses one's sins and who then offers forgiveness or advice.

confidant (*masc.*) or **confidante** (*fem.*), *n.* a person who is trusted with one's secrets, or with whom one discusses highly personal situations and problems.

confirmed bachelor. See BACHELOR.

conflict, *n.* 1. disagreement or opposition. 2. a battle.

conformity, *n.* 1. behavior that is similar to the majority in a group or society. 2. obedience to rules or social norms. 3. correspondence between two or more things: "Her behavior was in conformity with her beliefs."

confront, *v.* 1. come face-to-face in a defiant, argumentative, or hostile manner. 2. present someone with information in an argumentative or accusatory manner. 3. come face-to-face, especially suddenly. 4. acknowledge and attempt to deal with a problem or situation.

conjoined twins, twins born with their bodies connected to each other, often called **Siamese twins** after the famous brothers, Chang and Eng Bunker, who were born in Siam (Thailand) in 1811. Today the technical term, conjoined twins, is preferred.

conjugal, *adj.* having to do with the relationship between spouses. A **conjugal visit** is a private visit to a prisoner by the prisoner's spouse, typically including sexual relations. Most U.S. states do not allow this kind of visit.

connubial, *adj.* having to do with marriage.

consanguinity, *n.* kinship based on descent from a common ancestor. Formulas calculating degrees of consanguinity are used in legal contexts to determine inheritance and prohibit incest. **Lineal consanguinity** is a direct-line relationship, such as grandparent, parent, and child. **Coll-**

ateral consanguinity is a relationship between people who have a common ancestor but are not in a direct line with each other, such as uncles, aunts, and cousins. See COUSIN.

consensual, *adj.* existing or occurring by mutual consent.

consensus, *n.* a general agreement within a group.

conservator, *n.* 1. a guardian appointed by a judge to manage the daily care and/or financial affairs of a person who has been determined unable to care for himself or herself. 2. a person who takes care of the property of a museum, library, gallery, or estate.

conservatorship, *n.* 1. a court case in which a responsible person or group is appointed to manage the well-being and financial affairs of an adult who has been determined unable to care for himself or herself. 2. the state of being a conservator. 3. the state of being managed by a conservator.

consort, *n.* 1. a spouse, especially of a royal person. *v.* 2. associate or keep company, often used with a negative connotation.

consortium, *n.* 1. a group of businesses or business people cooperating in a large financial operation. 2. the legal right of marriage partners to each other's support, cooperation, and companionship.

conspire, *v.* 1. make plans to commit a wrongful act. 2. work together, especially in secret, for the same goal. 3. referring to events or circumstances: to occur together as if by design for a particular result, especially to someone's detriment.

consultant, *n.* someone who is hired to provide expert advice.

consummate, *v.* 1. make a marriage complete by engaging in sexual intercourse. 2. complete a business deal by signing a contract or fulfilling an obligation.

consummation, *n.* the act of consummating a marriage or completing a transaction.

contact, *n.* 1. the act or condition of touching. 2. communication or close association. 3. an acquaintance, colleague, or friend who may provide information or assistance. 4. someone whose name and email address, or other information such as phone numbers, are stored in a database or list. *v.* 5. communicate.

contact comfort, pleasure and reassurance derived from close physical contact with another. This is the basis of an infant's attachment with its caregiver.

contact hypothesis, *psych.* the theory that prejudice and conflict between groups can be reduced by interpersonal contact among members of the different groups.

contact list, a collection of names and phone numbers or email addresses.

contempt, *n.* 1. a feeling of scorn or disgust. 2. a view of someone or something as vile or worthless; a complete lack of respect for someone.

contested divorce, a divorce proceeding in which the parties disagree, either about getting divorced at all, or about the terms and conditions of the divorce. If the parties cannot reach a settlement, the court will eventually determine the outcome. An **uncontested divorce** is one in which the parties agree or reach a settlement without intervention from the court. An uncontested divorce may be the same as a **default divorce**, in which one party files the papers with the court and the other party simply fails to respond, resulting in the court granting all terms as requested by the filing party.

conversation, *n.* 1. communication via spoken words. 2. an informal exchange of information and ideas.

converse, *v.* participate in a conversation.

cooperate, *v.* 1. work together for a common purpose. 2. provide assistance in compliance with a request.

cooperation, *n.* the act or condition of working together or providing assistance.

cooperative, *adj.* 1. willing to cooperate. *n.* 2. a business jointly owned by its members, usually consumers or farmers, for their mutual benefit.

coquette, *n. French.* an ostentatiously flirtatious woman.

correspondence bias. See FUNDAMENTAL ATTRIBUTION ERROR.

cosset, *v. archaic.* pamper and coddle someone.

coterie, *n.* a small group of people closely associated with each other based on common interests.

cougar, *n. slang*. A woman who prefers to date or marry much younger men.

count on [someone], rely on or trust someone.

countertransference. See TRANSFERENCE.

countryman, countrywoman, *n.* 1. a person from one's own country. 2. a person who lives in the countryside.

couple, *n.* 1. two together; a pair. 2. two people established in a relationship, such as dating or marriage.

couples counseling, a type of psychotherapy intended to help couples resolve conflicts and improve their relationships. Also called **marriage counseling** or **marital therapy**. A professional who practices couples counseling is a **couples counselor** or **marriage counselor**.

court, *v.* 1. try to gain favor or attention. 2. seek affection; woo. *n.* 3. a place where legal decisions are made.

courtesy, *n.* 1. politeness; good social behavior. 2. a kind or considerate action. 3. a favor.

courtly love, a medieval concept of romantic love that was simultaneously spiritual, passionate, noble, and illicit. Popular from the 12th to 14th centuries, courtly love originated as a literary ideal emphasizing chivalry, and eventually developed into a stylized set of social practices among the nobility.

courtship, *n.* 1. attention paid by two people to each other with marriage as the goal; wooing. 2. the period of time during which such attention takes place. 3. in reference to animals: activities or rituals leading to mating or the formation of a pair bond.

cousin, *n.* a child or descendant of one's aunt or uncle (or great-aunt/great-uncle, etc.). Cousins are described numerically to indicate degrees of closeness, and by times "removed" to indicate different generations. Your first cousins share grandparents with you (they are the children of your aunts and uncles). Your second cousins share great-grandparents with you, but not grandparents. Third cousins have the same great-great-grandparents, but not the same great-grandparents.

And so on. A cousin "once removed" is one generation apart from you. Thus, your father's first cousin is your first cousin, once removed. Your grandfather's first cousin is your first cousin, twice removed. Note that in historical texts, "cousin" sometimes means a niece or nephew, or any distant relative. See CONSANGUINITY.

coven, *n.* a group of witches.

covenant marriage, a kind of marriage contract available as an option in a few states, which requires the marrying couple to undergo premarital counseling, and which strictly limits grounds for divorce.

coverture, *n. obs.* historically, the legal status of a married woman considered to be under the protection and authority of her husband.

covet, *v.* 1. strongly desire someone else's property or situation. 2. wish for a desirable item.

co-wife, another wife of one's husband. See POLYGAMY.

coworker, *n.* someone who works for the same organization.

crazy about [someone/something], extremely fond of someone or something.

crew, *n.* 1 group of persons involved in a particular type of work or working on the same project. 2. a group of people who work on a ship or boat. 3. a band of armed men. 4. *slang.* a group of friends or an entourage.

criminal conversation, historically, a legal term for seduction of another's spouse; adultery.

criticism, *n.* the expression of an unfavorable judgment or evaluation. **Constructive criticism** is criticism that is supposedly expressed in a helpful way.

criticize, *v.* find fault; express a negative evaluation.

crony, *n.* a close friend or companion. This term is often used with the connotation of getting into mischief together or being involved in conspiracies or corruption.

crush, *n.* 1. an infatuation. 2. a person who is the object of an infatuation.

cuckold, *n.* the husband of an adulterous wife. Derived from the name of the cuckoo, which lays its eggs in another bird's nest.

cuddle, *v.* hold someone close in an affectionate manner, especially while seated or lying down.

cupboard love, *idiom.* affection that is given in order to gain a reward, as when a child or pet behaves affectionately to get a treat.

Cupid, *n.* the ancient Roman god of love, often portrayed as a young, winged, naked boy with a bow and arrow. An arrow from Cupid's bow fired into someone's heart symbolizes falling in love. Identified with the Greek god Eros.

curry favor, *idiom.* use flattery and special attention in an effort to gain an advantage for oneself.

custodial care, in the context of health care: non-skilled personal assistance, such as help with bathing and other activities of daily living.

custodial parent, a parent who has custody of a child; the parent with whom the child lives all or most of the time.

custody, *n.* 1. protective care or guardianship. 2. imprisonment.

customer, *n.* one who purchases goods or services from another.

cute meet. See MEET CUTE.

cut [someone] off, 1. interrupt someone. 2. intercept or block someone's path. 2. terminate someone's financial support.

D

dad, *n. inf.* father.

daddy, nickname for dad.

daddy's girl, *coll.* a girl or young woman who is particularly attached to her father and is much indulged by him. See MAMA'S BOY.

Damon and Pythias, two great friends from classical mythology. Damon pledged his life to ensure the return of Pythias.

damsel in distress, a standard character in literature: a young woman in a terrible situation, who must be rescued by a hero.

dance attendance on, *idiom.* try to please someone by being available to meet all requests.

Darby and Joan, *British.* prototypical happily married, elderly couple. Based on a 1735 poem by Henry Woodfall and several subsequent poems by others.

darling, *n.* 1. a person who is very dear to another. 2. an endearment. *adj.* 3. much loved; precious.

date, *n.* 1. a social encounter arranged in advance, especially with a potential or current romantic partner. 2. the person with whom one goes on a date or attends a social function. *v.* 3. go out on dates with someone.

date night, 1. a night set aside by a couple, especially a couple with a well-established relationship, to go out together. 2. a night, such as Friday or Saturday, when it is common for people to go on dates.

date rape. See RAPE.

daughter, *n.* 1. one's female child. 2. a female descendant.

daughter-in-law, *pl.* daughters-in-law. *n.* the wife of one's child.

dead ringer, *idiom.* someone who looks exactly like another person.

dead to [someone], *idiom.* 1. completely ignored by someone, as if one did not exist. 2. disowned by someone.

dear, *adj.* 1. loved, cherished. 2. precious. 3. valuable or expensive. *n.* 4. one who is loved or cherished. 5. an endearment.

Dear John letter, *idiom.* a letter from a woman to her husband or boyfriend, especially to a serviceman overseas, terminating their relationship, often because she has found someone new. The phrase most likely originated during World War II.

defame, *v.* attack someone's reputation with malicious falsehoods.

default divorce. See CONTESTED DIVORCE.

defendant, *n.* the party who is accused in a lawsuit or criminal complaint.

defensiveness, *n.* behavior designed to protect oneself from criticism and justify one's actions, especially when one feels anger, anxiety, or guilt.

deferential, *adj.* respectful.

defiance, *n.* resistance to authority or opposition.

defiant, adj. showing bold opposition or disobedience.

defy, *v.* 1. refuse to obey. 2. challenge someone to do something that seems impossible.

deindividuation, *n. psych.* a loss of the sense of personal responsibility or accountability when one is part of a crowd or experiences anonymity in a group or online. Often associated with violent or antisocial behavior.

delegate, *v.* assign a task or responsibility to another. *n.* 2. someone who is authorized to represent or act on behalf of another.

dependent, in reference to a person: *n.* 1. someone whose financial support is provided by another, especially a child or other family member. *adj.* 2. needing something or someone else for assistance or support.

dependent personality disorder, *psych.* an emotional disorder characterized by a lack of self-confidence, difficulty making decisions, and fear of being alone.

descendant, *n.* someone who has come from a particular line of ancestors, or whose ancestor is a particular person.

descend from, have a particular person or family as one's ancestors.

detractor, *n.* one who disparages someone or something.

devotion, *n.* loyal dedication.

dialogue, *n.* 1. a conversation involving two or more people. 2. an exchange of ideas between differing individuals or groups.

diamond anniversary or **diamond wedding**, a couple's 75th wedding anniversary. Diamond anniversary sometimes refers to the 60th anniversary and all others from that point on.

differentiation, *n. psych.* the process of perceiving oneself as an autonomous entity.

diffusion of responsibility, *psych.* a phenomenon in which individuals are less likely to take responsibility when others are present. See BYSTANDER EFFECT, DEINDIVIDUATION.

dis, **diss**. *v. slang.* insult someone. Shortened form of "disrespect".

disagreement, *n.* 1. a lack of agreement. 2. an argument or quarrel.

disband, *v.* dissolve an organization; stop functioning as a group.

discuss, *v.* 1. talk or write about something in detail. 2. talk about something with a person or group.

discussion, *n.* the act of discussing.

disinherit, *v.* exclude someone from an inheritance or birthright.

disown, *v.* 1. refuse to acknowledge or maintain any connection with someone. 2. deny any ownership or responsibility. 3. repudiate a family relationship. 4. disinherit.

dispute, *v.* 1. engage in an argument. 2. argue against something. *n.* 3. an argument or debate.

disrespect, *n.* 1. rudeness, lack of respect. *v.* 2. treat someone rudely or contemptuously.

dissolution of marriage, divorce.

distrust, *n.* 1. suspicion or lack of trust. *v.* 2. regard someone with suspicion or without trust.

divorce, *n.* the legal termination of a marriage. In some jurisdictions, a divorce that ends the marriage is known as an absolute divorce, while a legal separation, in which the partners are still technically married (and cannot remarry), is known as a limited divorce. See GROUNDS FOR DIVORCE, LEGAL SEPARATION, NO-FAULT DIVORCE.

divorcée (*fem.*), **divorcee** (*fem.* or *masc.*), **divorcé** (*masc.*), *n.* a person who is divorced.

divorce mill, 1. a jurisdiction where divorces are very easily obtained. 2. a divorce court in such a place.

doctor, *n.* 1. a person licensed to practice medicine. 2. in academic circles, a person who has earned a PhD. *v.* 3. give medical treatment or first aid.

dog in the manger, *idiom.* a person who selfishly prevents others from having or using something even though he has no need for it himself. From an Aesop fable about a dog lying in a manger of hay who snapped at a hungry ox trying to eat.

domestic, *adj.* having to do with the home, household, or family.

domestic abuse, an incident or pattern of abusive behavior or violence that is used by one person to gain or maintain power and control over an intimate partner or family member.

domestic partner, someone who cohabits with another. In some cases an unmarried couple may be able to register their domestic partnership with an employer or agency in order to receive some of the financial and social benefits of marriage. See CIVIL UNION.

domestic violence. See DOMESTIC ABUSE.

dominance, *n*. 1. control, authority, or power over others. 2. high status or achievement in a particular field or endeavor.

dominate, *v*. 1. control or have authority over. 2. be the major force or most outstanding participant in a particular situation or endeavor. 3. bully.

Don Juan, *n*. a man who compulsively flirts and seduces women but lacks the capacity to experience love; a philanderer. From the fictional character Don Juan, who appeared in a number of legends and stories, and was portrayed in an opera by Mozart.

doppelgänger, doppelganger, *n. German.* a ghostly duplicate of a living person.

double bed, a bed large enough to accommodate two adults, also known as a **full-size bed.**

double cross, cheat or betray a colleague or friend.

double cousins, cousins who share all four grandparents; the offspring of a pair of brothers who married a pair of sisters, or of a brother and sister who married a sister and brother.

double date, a social event in which two couples go out together.

double wedding, a wedding ceremony in which two different couples are married at the same time or consecutively.

dowry, *n*. money and property that a woman brings to her husband upon marriage, or that her family provides to the husband or his family. See BRIDE PRICE.

doyen, *n*. 1. the most respected or outstanding person in a particular field. 2. the senior member of a group.

drift apart, 1. gradually lose feelings of closeness with someone. 2. lose contact with someone over time. 3. become alienated from someone.

droit du seigneur, *French.* supposedly the right of a feudal lord in medieval Europe to have sexual intercourse with the brides of his vassals on their wedding night. Almost certainly a myth.

drop in on, visit informally or unexpectedly.

dual-career marriage, a marriage in which both partners are wage earners.

duenna, *n*. in Spain and Portugal, a mature woman who serves as a chaperone for a girl or young woman.

dump [someone], *idiom*. end a relationship or fire someone from a job in a sudden, unkind manner.

duo, *n*. 1. two people closely associated with each other. 2. in music, a duet. 3. a couple.

Dutch treat, *idiom*. an event or date where each person pays his or her own way.

Dutch uncle, *idiom*. a man who provides severe advice or criticism.

dyad, *n*. a group of two.

dysfunctional, *adj*. malfunctioning; not working properly.

dysfunctional family, a family in which conflict, misbehavior, and neglect or abuse are perpetrated by one or both parents on a regular basis, leading other family members to accommodate them and adapt to the situation. Children in dysfunctional families often grow up thinking such behavior is normal.

dysfunctional relationship, a relationship in which people interact in ways that perpetuate their emotional problems and promote self-destructive behavior.

E

egalitarian, *adj*. characterized by a belief in the equality of all people.

egalitarian marriage, a marriage in which the partners share equally in domestic chores, child care, household decisions, and financial decisions, and in which equal importance is placed on each partner's career and personal goals.

elder, *n*. 1. a person who is older than oneself. 2. a person of advanced age. 3. a senior officer or functionary in an organization. 4. a wise and influential person in a tribe or community.

elder abuse, abusive, harmful, or negligent acts perpetrated against an older person, especially one who is frail, vulnerable, or dependent.

Electra complex. See OEDIPUS COMPLEX

elope, *v*. run off and get married secretly or suddenly.

embrace, *v*. 1. hold someone or something in one's arms. 2. accept eagerly. *n*. 3. the act or condition of embracing.

emotion, *n*. 1. a state of mind derived from one's feelings or mood, as distinguished from cognition or simple awareness. 2. a feeling such as sorrow, joy, love, hate, or fear, typically accompanied by certain physiological reactions and sensations.
    Scientific research has identified six basic emotions that are expressed the same way by all humans regardless of culture: happiness, sadness, fear, anger, surprise, and disgust.

emotional affair. See AFFAIR.

emotional attunement, the ability to recognize another's emotions, feelings, and moods, and to respond in an empathetic or appropriate manner.

emotionally focused therapy (EFT), a type of couples therapy that is guided by the science of attachment theory. EFT is also used with individuals and families.

empathy, *n.* the ability to identify with or vicariously experience another's thoughts, feelings, emotions, and attitudes.

employee, *n.* someone who is paid to work for another person or a business.

employer, *n.* a person or business that pays people for work.

empty nest syndrome, *idiom.* emotional reactions experienced by parents whose children all have grown up and left home. An **empty-nester** is a parent whose children have left home.

emulate, *v.* imitate, especially with the intention to equal or surpass.

enabler, *n.* 1. a person or thing that makes something possible. 2. someone who encourages or assists another's self-destructive behavior.

enamored, *adj.* 1. charmed or infatuated with someone. 2. fascinated or obsessed with something.

endearment, *n.* 1. an action or utterance that shows affection 2. an affectionate nickname.

endogamy, *n.* marriage within one's specific ethnic, social, or kinship group. See EXOGAMY.

enemy, *n.* 1. one who feels hatred for another. 2. an adversary or opponent. 3. an opposing military force.

engagement, *n.* 1. a betrothal; a promise to marry. 2. the period of time between an agreement to marry and the wedding.

engagement ring, a ring, typically given by a man to his fiancée, to symbolize their commitment to marry. Engagement rings often contain precious stones, such as diamonds. Traditions and customs surrounding engagement rings vary among cultures. See PROMISE RING, WEDDING RING.

enmeshment, *n. psych.* a dysfunctional relationship between two or more people, especially a family, in which personal boundaries are unclear or nonexistent, and autonomy and individuality are suppressed.

enmity, *n.* 1. a feeling of hostility or antagonism. 2. the state of being an enemy.

enthrall, *v*. 1. fascinate or charm; capture someone's full attention. 2. enslave someone psychologically.

entourage, *n*. a group of attendants or associates surrounding or traveling with a high-ranking person.

envy, *n*. 1. a feeling of resentment or jealousy triggered by another's advantages or superiority. 2. covetousness; the desire to have what someone else has.

equitable distribution law, a law governing the way a court divides property between spouses who divorce, if they are unable to come to an agreement outside of court.

Eros, *n*. 1. The Greek god of love, identified with the Roman god Cupid. 2. when spelled with lower case: sexual love or the libido.

erotomania, *n. psych*. a delusional disorder in which an individual believes that another (usually someone of higher social status) is in love with the individual. Erotomania sometimes leads to harassment and stalking.

escort, *n*. 1. a person or group that accompanies another for purposes of security, guidance, or courtesy. 2. someone who accompanies another to an event, especially a male who accompanies a female. 3. a person who is hired to accompany another to an event. 4. a person who is paid to date someone, typically including a sexual relationship. *v*. 5. accompany someone.

esteem, *n*. 1. a highly favorable opinion; respect. 2. *archaic*. judgment or opinion. *v*. 2. feel admiration and respect.

estranged, *adj*. 1. alienated from someone with whom one had a friendship or family relationship. 2. no longer having communication with someone.

et tu Brute?, a Latin phrase meaning "even you, Brutus?" used to express surprise and dismay at a friend's betrayal. Reported by Suetonius in *Lives of the Caesars* (121 AD) as Julius Caesar's last words, and popularized by William Shakespeare's play *Julius Caesar*.

etiquette, *n*. 1. a code of social behavior, especially regarding specific events or activities. 2. a prescribed or standard system of ceremonial behavior. 3. politeness. 4. norms of ethical behavior among professionals.

ex, *n. coll.* a former spouse or romantic partner. Shortened form of ex-husband, ex-girlfriend, etc.

exogamy, *n.* marriage outside of one's ethnic or social group. See ENDOGAMY.

extended family. See FAMILY.

extramarital, *adj.* outside of marriage.

extrovert, *n.* someone with an outgoing personality who feels energized by social contact.

eye contact, the act of looking at someone else's eyes.

F

face, *n.* 1. anatomically, the face is the front part of the head. 2. a look or expression: "He had a sad face." 3. a person who speaks for or represents a group or organization: "She was the face of Widgets, Inc."

To **wear a face** of some kind is to display a mood or emotion: "He always wore a happy face." To **put on a face** of some kind is to intentionally show a mood or attitude: "Despite the threats, she put on a bold face." (However, to **put on one's face** or **put one's face on** means to apply makeup.) To **make a face** is to scowl or show distaste. To **make faces** is to intentionally contort one's expression, typically to tease someone or to be funny. To **set one's face against** something is to oppose it. To **show one's face** is to make an appearance somewhere. To perform an action **to one's face** is to do it directly or boldly: "She insulted me to my face." To be **in [someone]'s face** is to be physically close while speaking or behaving in an aggressive or intimidating manner.

face, *n. soc.* a person's self-image in the context of public approval and respect. To **lose face** is to be publicly embarrassed or lose others' respect. To **save face** is to avoid humiliation. Politeness theories developed by sociolinguists Penelope Brown and Stephen Levinson distinguish between **positive face** (the desire for respect and liking) and **negative face** (the desire not to be bothered), and define some types of speech as **face-threatening acts**.

face, *v.* 1. be positioned toward something or someone. 2. position oneself to look at or toward something or someone. 3. acknowledge and deal with something: "We must face our fears." 4. confront. 5. **face up to** something, acknowledge and deal with a problem or challenge. 6. **be faced with** something, be confronted by or presented with a problem or challenge. 7. **face [someone] down**, confront someone with determination until that person gives way. 8. **face off**, confront someone in a competition.

face-off, faceoff, *n.* a direct confrontation.

face to face, 1. turned toward each other 2. directly confronting.

failed marriage, a marriage that ended in divorce.

fair-haired boy, *idiom*. the favorite, especially at work. Also **blue-eyed boy**.

fair weather friend, *idiom*. someone who is a friend only when it is convenient.

fairy godmother, a stock character in children's literature, a female with magical powers who aids the protagonist. Sometimes used to describe someone who provides generous, unexpected assistance.

faithful, *adj*. 1. loyal. 2. keeping one's promises. 3. following a procedure or rule thoroughly or strictly.

fall for, *idiom*. develop romantic feelings for. (However, to fall for something often means to be fooled, and the phrase **fall for it** always means to be fooled.)

fall guy, scapegoat.

falling-out, *n*. an argument or estrangement between people who were previously close. (However, **fallout** is the dust and particles that settle after an explosion, or the negative consequences of an incident.)

fall in love, 1. develop a strong emotional bond. 2. become infatuated.

fall in with, *idiom*. become associated with.

fall out with, *idiom*. become unfriendly with.

familiar, *adj*. 1. well-acquainted with someone or something. 2. well-known or commonly seen. 3. informal. 4. close or intimate. *n*. 5. a demon believed to serve a witch, often in the form of a pet animal, also called a **familiar spirit**.

familiarity breeds contempt, *proverb*. People in close association are likely to lose respect for each other. Possibly originated in Aesop's tale, "The Fox and the Lion."

family, *n*. 1. a group of two or more people related by blood, marriage, or adoption. 2. parents and their children. 3. all the people who are descended from a common ancestor. 4. a group of people (and sometimes pets) who form a household. 5. a group of people who feel bonded with each other by virtue of having shared significant life experiences.
    A **nuclear family** is a social unit consisting of parents and their children. **Immediate family** refers to one's closest relatives, usually

one's spouse, children, and parents. **Extended family** refers to relatives beyond the nuclear or immediate family, including grandparents, aunts and uncles, and cousins. A **blended family** is a family consisting of a couple with children from one or more previous relationships, as well as from the current relationship. **Stepfamily** is another name for blended family.

family dynamics, the patterns of interactions within a family.

family name, 1. the hereditary surname of a family. 2. a family's reputation. 3. a given name frequently used within an extended family or by succeeding generations.

family of orientation, *soc.* family of origin.

family of origin, the family in which one grew up, usually the family of one's birth or one's adoptive family.

family of procreation, *soc.* one's spouse and children.

family reunion, an event where many members of an extended family gather.

family therapy, a type of therapy in which the therapist sees two or more family members at the same time.

family ties, connections or bonds between relatives.

family tree, a genealogical chart showing the relationships of family members.

famulus, *n. obs.* the servant or assistant of a scholar or magician.

fan, *n.* an enthusiastic follower or devotee. Derived from *fanatic.*

father, *n.* 1. a male parent. 2. a male ancestor or founder. 3. a priest. *v.* 4. become the father of a child. 5. care for someone as a father or in a paternal manner.

father figure, 1. a man who appears to embody the characteristics of an idealized father. 2. a male relative or friend who provides a role model for a child, especially a child whose father is dead or absent. 3. a mother or female caretaker who attempts to fill a missing father's role.

fatherhood, *n.* the state of being a father.

father-in-law, *pl.* fathers-in-law. *n.* the father of one's spouse.

Father's Day, a holiday for the purpose of honoring fathers, celebrated in the U.S. on the third Sunday of June.

favor, *n.* 1. an act of special kindness or courtesy. 2. an attitude of good will or approval. 3. the state of being approved of. 4. a small gift or token, especially one distributed at a party or other event. *v.* 5. prefer or give preferential treatment. 6. comply with a request or perform a kind action. 7. resemble someone, especially a parent.
       To be **in favor** is to be preferred or in fashion. To be **in favor of** something is to be supportive. To **find favor** is to be liked. To **fall out of favor** is to lose acceptance or popularity. To **show favor** is to give kind or preferential treatment.

favoritism, *n.* a strong preference for one person or thing over another; preferential treatment.

fellow, *n.* 1. a man or boy. 2. a companion. 3. someone in the same occupation or condition. 4. a graduate student who has received a grant for special studies. 5. *inf.* a person. *adj.* 6. sharing the same occupation, activity, interests, or condition; belonging to the same group: fellow citizens, fellow students.

fellow creature, another living being.

fellow man/woman/human, another human being, especially one sharing similar conditions or feelings.

fellowship, *n.* 1. friendly companionship. 2. a community or organization of persons sharing similar feelings and interests. 3. a position of special study in an educational institution, supported by a stipend or allowance.

fellow traveler, someone who sympathizes with or supports the goals of a political party, especially the Communist party.

femme fatale, an irresistibly attractive woman, especially one who leads men into danger or difficulty. French, meaning "fatal woman."

feral child, a child raised in isolation without normal exposure to human contact, socialization, and, most significantly, language. Often these children have been confined and abused or neglected by their parents. In some cases they have been abandoned or lost in the wild at an early age, and may have lived with animals. Once rescued, they typically have difficulty integrating into society and may never develop normal language skills.

feud, *n.* 1. an intense, ongoing hostility between two families or clans. 2. a heated disagreement or quarrel between two groups or factions. *v.* 3. engage in ongoing hostility.

fiancé (*masc.*) or **fiancée/fiancee** (*fem.*), *n.* a person to whom one is engaged. In recent years, some people have begun to extend this word to refer to a person with whom one cohabits and has children, without any plan to marry.

fictive kinship, *anth.* a relationship modeled after kinship, based on social customs rather than genetic relationships or marriage.

fidelity, *n.* faithfulness.

fiduciary, *n.* a person, such as an executor or trustee, who is entrusted to manage money or property for the benefit of another.

fifth wheel, *idiom.* a superfluous or unnecessary person or thing.

fight, *n.* 1. battle or combat. 2. a violent altercation. 3. an angry argument or disagreement. 4. a boxing match. 5. the energy needed to engage in a struggle. *v.* 6. participate in a fight or argument. 7. struggle against something, such as temptation or a disease. 8. fiercely promote or work for something, such as a social cause.

filial, *adj.* 1. pertaining to a son or daughter. 2. having the relationship of a child to a parent.

first impression, a mental image or opinion formed about someone or something the first time one encounters that person or thing.

first lady, the wife of a head of state.

flatmate, *n. British.* roommate.

flatter, *v.* compliment someone effusively, especially in a way that is exaggerated or insincere.

flesh and blood, *idiom.* 1. a relative or relatives. 2. the human body, especially in contrast to something spiritual or imaginary: "My dream came true when I met a flesh-and-blood princess."

fling, *n.* a brief romantic relationship.

flirt, *v.* playfully show sexual or romantic interest, often without serious intentions.

foe, *n.* enemy.

foil, *n.* a person who makes another seem better or smarter by contrast.

follow, *v.* 1. move or travel behind someone. 2. come after in time or order. 3. accept someone as a guide or leader; accept someone's authority. 4. obey instructions. 5. imitate or copy. 6. pay close attention to someone's actions, career, or life. 7. regularly read or subscribe to a blog or other social media outlet.

follower, *n.* 1. someone who follows. 2. a fan or subscriber.

fond, *adj.* feeling affection or liking toward someone or something.

fondle, *v.* 1. touch someone or something in an affectionate manner. 2. caress in an erotic manner.

football widow. See SPORTS WIDOW.

foot-in-the-door phenomenon, *idiom.* the tendency to agree to a difficult request if one has previously agreed to an easy one. Derived from the idea that a salesman who can manage to get his foot in the door improves his chances of making a sale.

for better or worse, *idiom.* a phrase excerpted from traditional wedding vows, indicating a promise to be loyal under all circumstances.

for better or worse, but not for lunch, *proverb.* A wife would prefer that her husband not spend the entire day at home with her. Usually in reference to a husband who has retired and may interfere with his wife's daily routine.

forced marriage, a form of slavery in which an unwilling person (almost always female) is forced into marriage, often through kidnapping, by intimidating her family, or in exchange for money paid to her family. Forced marriages typically involve rape and other abuses of the victim. Forced marriage is sometimes called **marriage by capture**, **marriage by abduction**, **bride kidnapping**, and similar terms. See CHILD MARRIAGE.

forefather, foremother, *n.* an ancestor.

forgive, *v.* 1. grant a pardon or absolve someone of blame. 2. give up all claims for compensation or retribution. 3. cease feeling anger and resentment. 4. release someone from a debt.

forgiveness, *n.* 1. the act of forgiving. 2. the state of being forgiven. 3. willingness to forgive.

foster, *v.* 1. promote the growth and development of someone or something. 2. bring up a child that is not one's own. 3. care for a homeless pet until a home can be found for it.

foster home, a temporary or permanent home in which one or more children are raised by someone who is not their parent. **foster child,** a child being raised by someone other than its own parent. **foster parent,** an adult who acts as a mother or father to a foster child. **foster brother, foster sister,** a child brought up in a foster home with children from different parents. See ADOPTION.

four horsemen of the Apocalypse, a concept developed by psychologist John Gottman to describe four key symptoms of a marriage that is at risk of divorce: criticism, contempt, defensiveness, and stonewalling. Derived from four horsemen mentioned in the Bible, popularly viewed as symbolizing disasters accompanying the end of the world.

foursome, *n.* 1. a golf match between two pairs of people. 2. a group consisting of two couples. 3. a group of four.

frat boy, 1. derogatory term for a member of a fraternity. 2. a young male, especially in college, whose behavior embodies negative stereotypes of privileged, obnoxious fraternity members.

fraternal, *adj.* 1. pertaining to brothers. 2. brotherly.

fraternal polyandry, a form of polygamy in which a woman is married to two or more brothers. Also called **adelphic polyandry.**

fraternal society, a membership organization, usually of men, organized for social, business, religious, or charitable activities.

fraternity, *n.* 1. an organization of male students. 2. a group or class of people having common purposes and interests. 3. a quality or feeling of being brotherly; brotherhood.

fraternize, *v*. associate with someone or form a friendship, particularly in a situation where the relationship is inappropriate or forbidden, such as with a subordinate at work or with the enemy during war.

freeloader, *n*. someone who imposes on others for free food or other benefits.

free love, *idiom. archaic.* the concept or practice of engaging in sexual relationships as desired, without the restrictions of marriage or other commitments.

freeze [someone] out, *idiom.* exclude or ignore someone.

frenemy, *n. slang,* a person who appears as a friend despite an underlying dislike or rivalry. Coined in the 1950s, probably by Walter Winchell, by combining "friend" and "enemy".

Friday. See MAN FRIDAY.

friend, *n*. 1. a person one knows and for whom one feels an attachment based on affection or admiration. 2. someone who is on good terms with another; a companion or confidant. 3. someone who is supportive of an organization or a cause. *v*. 4. *coll.* add someone to one's contact list on a social media website. 5. **befriend**, become someone's friend. 6. **make friends**, become friends with one or more people.

friend in need is a friend indeed, a, *proverb.* True friends help each other in times of difficulty.

friendly, *adj*. 1. pleasant and sociable. 2. kind and helpful. 4. not hostile. 4. **user-friendly**, in reference to books, software, tools, and devices: easy to understand and use.

friendship, *n*. 1. the state of being friends. 2. friendly feelings.

friendship ring, a ring given to a close friend as a token of affection. There are no cultural traditions regarding friendship rings, which may be made of any material, and are often hand made by the giver. They may be worn on any finger or as a pendant on a chain.

friends with benefits, *slang.* people who consider themselves friends without any romantic involvement, yet who engage in sexual relations with each other as a matter of convenience.

full-size bed See DOUBLE BED.

fundamental attribution error, *psych.* the tendency to attribute other people's behavior to their personality or character (especially character flaws) and not the situation, even when the situation is the most likely explanation. Also known as **correspondence bias**.

G

gadfly, *n.* a person who constantly annoys others, especially within organizations, with complaints, questions, requests, ideas, etc. Derived from the name of a species of fly that annoys domestic animals.

game theory, the study of strategically interdependent behavior.

gamophobia, *n.* fear of marriage.

gang, *n.* 1. a group of people associated for criminal purposes. 2. a group of laborers. 3. a group of people closely associated for social purposes. 4. a group or band of people gathered together. *v.* 5. *idiom.* To **gang up on [someone]** is to unite for the purpose of opposing, fighting, or bullying someone.

gaslight, *v. idiom.* use deception and tricks to psychologically manipulate others until they doubt their own perceptions and sanity. Derived from the 1938 stage play *Gas Light* by Patrick Hamilton.

gay, *adj.* homosexual. Until the latter part of the 20th century, the primary meaning of this word was "happy" or "festive," but it is no longer used in that sense.

geisha, *n.* in Japan, a professional hostess trained to entertain men with song, dance, and conversation.

gender role, sex role.

gene, *n.* the basic physical unit of heredity, transferred from parent to offspring in the chromosome.

genealogy, *n.* 1. the study of ancestry and family history. 2. the record of an individual's or family's ancestry. 3. descent from an ancestor; lineage.

genetic, *adj.* pertaining to genes or heredity.

genetic parent, a parent whose sperm or egg was employed in the conception of a child, whether naturally or through a medical procedure.

genogram, *n.* a detailed family tree or diagram, especially one that includes medical history, personality traits, emotional relationships, and behavior patterns.

gentleman caller, *idiom.* a man who visits one's home or who escorts one on a date, with the implication that he is a potential boyfriend.

get along with, have good relationship with.

get a rise out of [someone], *idiom.* provoke a reaction from someone, especially anger or annoyance.

get even, retaliate.

get in [someone]'s hair, *idiom.* annoy or interfere with someone.

get on, get on with, *idiom.* have a good relationship. To get on can also mean to manage or survive: "Now that he is out of the hospital, he is getting on well." To **get on with [something]** or **get on with it** means to proceed with an action or task. (However, **get it on** is a slang term for having sexual intercourse.)

get [someone]'s goat, *idiom.* annoy or anger someone.

get together, meet, especially to meet informally.

get-together, *n.* an informal meeting or social occasion.

gestation, *n.* the period during which a fetus develops in the womb.

ghost, *n.* the soul or spirit of a dead person, believed to wander among the living.

ghost marriage, a tradition in Chinese culture, whereby a newly deceased woman is buried next to a man who died unmarried, so that he will not be alone in the afterlife. In other cases a living woman is married to the spirit of a deceased man so that she can become part of his family. See POSTHUMOUS MARRIAGE.

ghost writer, someone who is hired to write a book, article, speech, etc., for someone else, usually anonymously.

gift, something that is voluntarily given without payment; a present.

gigolo, *n.* a man who receives gifts or financial support from women in exchange for companionship and sexual attention.

girl Friday. See MAN FRIDAY.

girlfriend, *n.* 1. a female friend in the context of dating or romance. 2. a woman's platonic female friend.

give birth [to], bear a child. See CHILDBIRTH.

give one's word, *idiom.* make a serious promise.

given name, the personal name assigned to an individual, as distinct from a family name. Often called **first name**, and occasionally **Christian name**, from the practice of formally naming a baby at a baptismal ceremony. See SURNAME.

give [someone] a hand, *idiom.* help someone.

glad-hander, *n. idiom.* a person who is overly enthusiastic when meeting and greeting others.

glare, *v.* stare at someone in an angry way.

goat, *n.* slang. 1. scapegoat. 2. **old goat**, a lecherous man.

go back on one's word, *idiom.* break a promise.

godparent, godfather, godmother, *n.* 1. someone who presents a child at baptism and takes responsibility for the child's religious education. 2. a close family friend who agrees to be involved in a child's upbringing and moral guidance.

go dutch, *idiom.* share the expenses. See DUTCH TREAT.

gold digger, *idiom.* a person (usually a woman) who associates with or marries someone primarily for material gain.

golden anniversary or **golden wedding**, a couple's 50th wedding anniversary.

golden rule, a principle of ethical conduct, usually expressed as, "Do unto others as you would have them do unto you."

golf widow. See SPORTS WIDOW.

good egg, *idiom*. a person who is good natured and trustworthy.

good enough marriage, *psych*. the concept that people can be happy and fulfilled in imperfect marriages that do not necessarily meet all their wishes or expectations.

good enough mother, good enough parent, *psych*. a concept derived from the work of psychoanalyst D.W. Winnicott and further developed by others, which recognizes that parents are imperfect and cannot avoid frustrating and disappointing their children, and that this is a necessary part of a child's healthy development.

good fences make good neighbors, *proverb*. People get along better when they observe proper boundaries. Popularized by Robert Frost's 1914 poem "Mending Wall," which used the phrase ironically.

good Joe, *idiom*. a good-natured person.

good Samaritan, *idiom*. a person who voluntarily helps a stranger in need, especially someone who has been injured or stranded. From a Bible story about a Samaritan who helped a man who had been beaten and robbed.

good-time Charlie, *idiom*. an easygoing, sociable man, always looking for fun.

good will, 1. a friendly or kind attitude. 2. the positive reputation of a business, considered as a quantifiable asset.

goo-goo eyes, *idiom*. silly, amorous glances.

go out with, go somewhere with someone, especially on a date.

gossip, *n*. idle talk and rumors, particularly about private or personal aspects of other people's lives.

go steady, *idiom*. date one person exclusively.

Gottman, John, (b. 1942) Professor Emeritus of Psychology at the University of Washington and co-founder, with his wife, Dr. Julie Schwartz Gottman, of the Gottman Institute. Known for his extensive research on marriage. Gottman's work has widely influenced the couples counseling movement.

governess, *n*. a woman hired to educate and supervise a child.

grand-, a prefix indicating a relative two generations older or younger than one, such as a grandmother or grandson.

grandaunt, **granduncle**, *n.* the sibling of one's grandparent; synonym for great-aunt or great-uncle.

grandbaby, *n. inf.* grandchild.

grandma, **granmaw**, **granny**, **grammaw**, **grammy**, **nana**. Nicknames for grandmother.

grandpa, **granpaw**, **grampaw**, **gramps**, nicknames for grandfather.

grandparent, **grandfather**, **grandmother**, *n.* a parent of one's mother or father. Adding the prefix great- indicates a parent of one's grandparent (e.g. great-grandmother).

grass widow, **grass widower**, *idiom.* a person who is separated or divorced.

gray divorce, *idiom.* divorce among senior citizens.

great-, a prefix that precedes "grand" to indicate a relative three generations older or younger than one, such as a great-grandfather or great-granddaughter. Additional *great*s can be added to indicate additional generations, as in, "He was my great-great-grandfather". Numbers may also be used, as in, "I believe she was my 7th great-grandmother".

great-aunt, **great-uncle**, *n.* a grandaunt or granduncle. The sibling of one's great-grandparent is a great-grandaunt or great-granduncle.

green-eyed monster, *idiom.* jealousy. From a line in Shakespeare's play *Othello*.

greeting card, a notecard given to someone as a friendly or affectionate gesture, especially as part of a holiday or special occasion.

gregarious, *adj.* sociable; enjoying the company of people.

groom, *n.* a newly married man or a man about to be married. Shortened form of "bridegroom".

groomsman, *n.* a man who serves as a ceremonial attendant to the groom at his wedding. The chief attendant is the **best man**.

grounds for divorce, legally valid reasons for obtaining a divorce. In the past, a spouse seeking a divorce was usually required to show fault on the part of the other spouse. Adultery and abandonment were typical grounds for divorce. Currently in the U.S., all states recognize no-fault divorce, in which the grounds are simply irreconcilable differences or a breakdown of the marriage. Some may also require that the couple be separated for a specified period of time prior to divorce. Currently, the overwhelming majority of countries allow divorce under some circumstances. Many now allow no-fault divorce, while others still require some kind of fault and may impose additional restrictions.

group, *n.* in reference to people: 1. two or more people who have something in common. In sociology, a **primary group** is a small group characterized by close relationships. A **secondary group** is larger and characterized by more formal relationships. 2. two or more people who are clustered together in an area.

group dynamics, the behavioral and psychological processes involved when people interact with each other within a group.

groupie, *slang*. 1. an enthusiastic female fan of a musical performer or group who follows them on tour, especially with the hope of meeting them or having a sexual relationship with them. 2. an ardent fan of a celebrity.

group marriage. See POLYGAMY.

groupthink, *n.* the practice of seeking or enforcing consensus and harmony within a group in such a way that decision making is impaired and individual thinking and creativity are stifled. Groupthink sometimes creates an effect called **group polarization**, in which the group makes a decision that is more extreme than any member would make individually.

group wedding. See COLLECTIVE WEDDING.

grow apart, in reference to a friendship or romantic relationship: to gradually become estranged.

grown child. See ADULT CHILD.

grudge, *n.* a strong feeling of resentment, especially related to a specific situation or incident. To **hold a grudge** is to remain resentful over a past offense.

grudge match, a competition between rivals who have a history of animosity.

guard, *v.* 1. protectively watch over someone or something; keep safe from harm. 2. prevent escape by keeping close watch. 3. take some protective action or provide with protective equipment. 4. in sports, to take a position that impedes an opponent. *n.* 5. a person or group that watches, protects, or takes a protective position. 6. a protective or defensive attitude or posture.

guardian, *n.* 1. a person who is legally entrusted with the care and protection of the person and/or property of a minor or other person who is legally incapable of managing his own affairs. 2. a person who has been granted the legal rights and responsibilities of a parent. 3. a person who defends or protects.

guardian angel, 1. an angel or similar supernatural being believed to watch over and protect someone. 2. a person who provides guidance or protection in a timely fashion, especially when unexpected, saving another from harm.

guest, *n.* 1. a visitor at one's home. 2. someone who attends a social event. 3. someone who patronizes a restaurant, hotel, or other facility. 4. a customer in a store.

guide dog. See SERVICE ANIMAL.

gynophobia, *n.* fear of women.

H

haggle, *v.* bargain in a petty or argumentative manner.

half brother or **half sister,** a sibling with whom one has only one parent in common. See FAMILY, STEP-.

hand-holding, *n.* 1. the act of holding another's hand. 2. patient, detailed instructions and guidance provided to a customer or learner.

handler, *n.* in reference to public figures: a person who is employed to guide, advise, and monitor the behavior of a public figure, especially a politician.

handmaid, *n.* a female servant.

handshake, *n.* a gesture in which two people grasp hands. Used as a greeting, to express congratulations, to show support or solidarity, or to indicate agreement.

handshake agreement, an oral agreement based on trust between the parties, often confirmed by a handshake. Handshake agreements are often preliminary agreements that are followed by formal contracts. Handshake agreements may be legally enforceable under some circumstances, but typically rely on honor rather than law.

hand [someone] his/her walking papers, *idiom.* require someone to leave.

hang out, *idiom.* spend time with others, usually without any specific purpose. Sometimes shortened to **hang.**

happily ever after, *idiom.* a standard phrase used at the end of fairy tales to sum up the life of the protagonists following their marriage. Often used to describe the hopes of young couples, especially as shorthand for unrealistic expectations.

harass, *v.* persistently disturb, annoy, torment, or intimidate.

harassment, *n.* 1. systematic or repeated behavior that is intimidating, annoying, upsetting, or malicious. In a workplace, harassment is sometimes grounds for a lawsuit against the harasser or the employer. Some kinds of harassment may also be defined as STALKING. 2. **sexual harassment** is a form of workplace harassment or discrimination involving unwanted sexual advances, obscene remarks, or other offensive behavior of a sexual nature.

harem, *n.* 1. historically, a separate part of a Middle Eastern household reserved as a residence for the women. Also called a **seraglio**. 2. the occupants of a harem. 3. the wives of a polygamist. 4. *slang.* a group of women who are devotees of a particular man or who compose his entourage.

hate, *v.* 1. dislike someone intensely. 2. feel strong hostility toward someone or something. 3. be strongly unwilling to do something. *n.* 4. extreme dislike, aversion, or hostility.

hatred, *n.* hate.

have something in common, have shared interests and preferences, or to have a similar background and experiences.

hazing, *n.* abusive or humiliating treatment of newcomers, especially as an initiation ritual.

head honcho, *coll.* the person in charge of an organization or group. Derived from a Japanese word for leader.

head over heels, *idiom.* intensely in love; infatuated. Derived in the 18th century from *heels over head*, an older expression which meant upside-down.

heart balm acts, **heart balm statutes**, laws that abolish or limit lawsuits seeking damages for a broken heart, such as ALIENATION OF AFFECTION or BREACH OF PROMISE.

heartbreak, *n.* extreme emotional pain caused by loss, betrayal, or disappointment.

heartbreaker, *n.* 1. a situation that causes great distress. 2. an attractive person who behaves irresponsibly or unkindly in relationships, leading to grief. 3. an attractive person whose unattainability causes sorrow to others.

heartthrob, *n. idiom.* a person whose attractive appearance inspires infatuation.

heart-to-heart talk, *idiom*. a frank, intimate conversation.

heir, *n*. a person who inherits, or is entitled to inherit, some or all of the possessions of a deceased person.

heir apparent, 1. a person whose right to inherit cannot be overturned. 2. the person who is most likely to succeed to another's position.

helicopter parent, *idiom*. a parent who is overprotective, constantly monitoring and getting involved in the child's every activity, attempting to protect the child from all difficulties. The comparison is made to a helicopter which constantly hovers overhead.

helpmeet or **helpmate**, *n*. 1. a helpful companion. 2 a spouse.
    "Helpmeet" was coined by joining two separate words from the book of Genesis, which contains the phrase, "I will make an help meet for him." The meaning of "meet" in that context was "suitable"; the phrase referred to a suitable helper. After "helpmeet" had been coined, "meet" was often replaced with "mate" as a better synonym for "spouse".

henchman, *n*. 1. a subordinate or assistant of a criminal. 2. an unscrupulous supporter of a political leader or party.

henpecked, *adj*. dominated or habitually scolded by one's wife.

hereditary, *adj*. 1. passing naturally from parents to offspring. 2. legally or customarily transmitted through a line of descent.

hermit, *n*. a person who has withdrawn from society and lives in a solitary place.

hero (*masc.* or *fem.*), **heroine** (*fem.*), *n*. 1. a courageous or noble person whose actions have earned admiration. 2. a person who has rescued others from danger. 3. a highly admired person who serves as a role model. 4. the male protagonist in a story. 5. in mythology, a person with superhuman or divine powers.

hero worship. 1. great respect and admiration for a highly accomplished person. 2. excessive admiration for someone perceived as great.

heterosexual, *adj*. sexually attracted to members of the opposite sex.

hierarchy, *n*. 1. a system in which people or things are ranked one above the other. 2. a body of ecclesiastical officials organized by ranks. 3.

government by ecclesiastical rulers. 4. a government or ruling body organized by ranks.

high-maintenance, *coll.* needing a great deal of time, attention, and effort.

hired hand, a laborer, especially on a farm or ranch.

hireling, *n.* an unimportant employee.

hitched, *adj. slang.* married. Derived from the practice of hitching (fastening) two animals together to pull a burden.

hit it off, *idiom.* develop a rapport.

hit on [someone], *slang.* show sexual attraction or make sexual advances toward someone.

homicide, *n.* the killing of a human being. Special terms can be used, depending on the relationship between the killer and the killed: **patricide**, killing one's father; **matricide**, killing one's mother; **fratricide**, killing one's brother; **sororicide**, killing one's sister; **uxoricide**, killing one's wife; **infanticide**, killing a baby; **filicide**, killing one's own child; **suicide**, killing oneself. Homicide may or may not be a crime, depending on the circumstances of the killing (for example, accident or self defense). Criminal homicide is usually called **murder**, and may be broken down into various categories, depending on the jurisdiction. The most common categories are **first-degree murder**, **second-degree murder**, and **manslaughter**. Killing a person in self defense or in defense of another is sometimes call **justifiable homicide**. Deliberately carrying out a plan to kill someone is often called **assassination**, especially if the victim is a prominent person.

homie, homeboy, *slang.* an acquaintance from one's neighborhood.

homosexual, *adj.* sexually attracted to members of the same sex.

honeymoon, *n.* 1. a short trip taken by a newly married couple. 2. approximately the first month of a marriage. 3. a period of happiness and harmony in a relationship. 4. a period of harmony characteristic of a new relationship. 5. **second honeymoon**, a romantic vacation taken by a couple, usually after several years of marriage.

honeymoon is over, the, *idiom.* The pleasant beginning has ended.

honeymoon phase, 1. typically the early part of a romantic relationship, during which the partners experience happiness and harmony, and view each other in a highly positive way. 2. an early, happy period in any kind of relationship.

honorable intentions, motives that are honest and fair, without deception or hidden agendas. Historically, when applied to dating or courtship, this phrase meant that a man was interested in a woman as a potential marriage partner and would not attempt to seduce her.

honorific, *n.* a title or grammatical form used to convey respect or honor when speaking to or about someone.

honor killing, *idiom.* in some cultures, the murder of a relative, almost always a female, who is accused of having dishonored the family in some way. Some of the reasons for these murders are refusal to accept an arranged marriage, having a boyfriend, getting a job, being the victim of rape, or dressing in ways that family members consider inappropriate. Murders of this kind occur in cultures where males obsessively control the lives of females, or where females are considered the property of their families.

hook [someone] up with [someone/something], *idiom.* arrange a meeting or help someone establish a connection.

hook up, *v.* inf. 1. meet. 2. *slang.* engage in casual sex.

hookup, *n.* 1. a connection, as between electrical wires. 2. *slang.* casual sex; a one-night stand.

hospitality, *n.* 1. friendly reception and treatment of guests. 2. the business of housing and entertaining visitors.

host (*masc.* or *fem.*), **hostess** (*fem.*), *n.* 1. a person who receives or entertains guests. 2. someone who pays for all or part of an entertainment or event. 3. an employee who greets restaurant patrons or who oversees the comfort of guests or passengers. *v.* 4. receive or entertain guests. 5. pay for all or part of an event or entertainment.

hostage, *n.* a person kidnapped and held prisoner in order to compel someone to fulfill certain demands, or to ensure the security of the captor.

hostile, *adj.* unfriendly, especially in an aggressive manner.

houseguest, *n.* a person who stays overnight as a guest in a household.

household, *n.* 1. a house and all its contents and occupants. *adj.* 2. pertaining to a home; belonging to or used in a house.

housewarming, *n.* a party celebrating the occupancy of a new home.

housewife, househusband, *n.* a spouse who has the primary responsibility for managing the household while the other spouse works at an income-producing job.

hubby, *n.* an affectionate abbreviation of "husband".

hug, *v.* 1. clasp one's arms around another person. *n.* 2. the act or state of hugging.

human trafficking. See SLAVERY.

humor [someone], accommodate a mood or comply with a whim in order to soothe or satisfy someone.

husband, *n.* a married man.

hypergamy, *n.* the practice of marrying someone who has higher social status than oneself. Commonly referred to as **marrying up**.

hypogamy, *n.* the practice of marrying someone of lower status than oneself. Commonly referred to as **marrying down**.

I

I do, in a traditional wedding ceremony, the customary response to being formally asked to take someone as a spouse.

illegitimate, *adj.* 1. illegal or improper. 2. born to unmarried parents. Historically, so-called illegitimate children were often subject to negative consequences such as the loss of the right to paternal support, inability to inherit, and social ostracism. In the U.S. and Europe this concept is now considered archaic, and the term "illegitimate child" is rarely used.

ill will, hostile or negative feelings.

imaginary friend, a psychological phenomenon in which a friendship takes place in a child's imagination. Although children may discuss their imaginary companions as if they were real, most seem to understand that they are imaginary.

impersonate, *v.* pretend to be another person, either as entertainment or for fraudulent purposes.

impostor, *n.* someone who assumes another's identity.

inbreeding, *n.* producing offspring from very closely related individuals. See INCEST.

incest, *n.* 1. sexual relations between people who are very closely related. 2. the crime of marriage or sexual relations between closely related people.
    Exactly which relationships are forbidden has changed throughout history and still varies culturally. Some ancient societies permitted marriages between siblings or half-siblings, particularly among royal families. In other cases, the incest taboo was extended to include many people not related by blood, but with a family connection, such as a deceased spouse's sibling, a stepparent, or step-sibling. Today, sexual relations between siblings or between parent (or grandparent) and child are universally considered incestuous. Uncle-niece and aunt-nephew marriages are prohibited in most places, but allowed in others (including at least two U.S. states). In the U.S. today, slightly more than half the states prohibit or limit marriages between first cousins. In some places, any sexual relationship (but not necessarily marriage) between consenting adults, no matter how closely related, is legal. Sexual relations between adults

and minor children, related or not, constitute criminal child sexual abuse.

incest taboo, *anth.* the prohibition against sexual relations between closely related individuals.

in common. See HAVE SOMETHING IN COMMON.

in crowd, *idiom.* a small group of people perceived as fashionable or popular.

incubus, *n.* a demon or evil spirit believed to appear in male form and engage in sexual intercourse with women as they sleep. See SUCCUBUS.

infant, *n.* a very young baby, usually under a year old.

infatuation, *n.* an all-absorbing passion for someone or something, typically characterized by irrational thinking and foolish behavior.

infidelity, *n.* unfaithfulness; adultery.

ingrate, *n.* someone who lacks gratitude and appreciation for the kindness and generosity of others.

ingroup, *n. soc.* a social group one strongly identifies with, especially an exclusive group that views outsiders as inferior or in opposition.

inherit, *v.* 1. receive property by succession or as specified in a will. 2. receive genetic characteristics from one's parents or ancestors. 3. be left with things or situations from a predecessor or previous owner.

inheritance, *n.* 1. property that passes to an heir or successor. 2. genetic characteristics transmitted to offspring.

in-laws, *n. pl.* people who are related by marriage rather than blood. For example, a spouse's mother is a mother-in-law.

in love, 1. having feelings of deep affection for someone. 2. infatuated. 3. having a strong emotional attachment or devotion to someone or something.

instruct, *v.* 1. give directions or orders. 2. provide facts about a particular topic. 3. teach or train.

insubordination, *n.* defiance of authority; refusal to follow orders.

insult, *n*. 1. a contemptuously rude remark or action. 2. an affront. *v*. 3. make a contemptuous remark or action.

intended, *n. archaic*. one's fiancé or fiancée.

interaction, *n*. the reciprocal effects or influences that people, groups, or things have on each other.

interdependence, *n*. mutual dependence between two or more people or things.

interlocutor, *n*. 1. someone who participates in a conversation. 2. someone who interrogates or conducts an interview.

internecine, *adj*. having to do with a vicious, mutually destructive conflict within a group.

interpersonal, *adj*. having to do with the relationships and interactions between people.

interrogate, *v*. 1. ask questions in an aggressive or detailed manner, especially when the person being asked considers the questions intrusive. 2. question someone in a formal setting, especially related to law enforcement.

intervention, *n. psych*. a process in which a group of people confront an addict, with the intention of triggering change and providing help.

interview, *n*. 1. a meeting in which one or more people ask questions of another in order to gather information for a news story, broadcast, or other report. 2. a meeting in which one or more people question or evaluate another for a specific purpose, such as employment.

in the doghouse, *idiom*. temporarily in trouble, especially with one's spouse or family members.

in the family way, *idiom, archaic*. euphemism for being pregnant.

in the flesh, *idiom*. present and visible: "I didn't think John would come, but there he was, in the flesh."

intimacy, *n*. 1. a close, familiar, and usually affectionate relationship. 2. a close association or detailed familiarity with a place or subject. 3. behavior indicating closeness or familiarity. 4.sexual behavior.

intimate, *adj*. 1. pertaining to a close personal relationship. 2. private; extremely personal. 3. associated with the feelings of a close relationship or warm friendship. 4. having cozy or comfortable characteristics. 5. sexual.

introduce, *v*. 1 to present people to each other in order to make them acquainted. 2. present someone or something to the public for the first time. 3. provide someone with some knowledge or an experience for the first time. 4. propose a new idea. 5. preface a speech or text.

introvert, *n*. a quiet or thoughtful person who generally prefers socializing only in small groups and having a certain amount of solitude or privacy.

intrude, *v*. 1. put oneself into a situation or a place where one is unwanted or uninvited. 2. enter a place illegally.

intruder, *n*. one who intrudes.

invade [someone]'s space, 1. get physically very close to someone, causing the person to feel uncomfortable or threatened. 2. enter an area that another person considers private.

invitation, *n*. 1. a spoken or written request to attend or participate in an event. 2. the act of inviting. 3. behavior or circumstances that make a particular action or outcome seem likely: "His behavior was an invitation to lawsuits."

invite, *v*. 1. make a polite request that someone attend or participate in an event. 2. make a formal request for something, such as a written opinion or a job application. 3. stimulate or incite a particular response: "His behavior invites criticism."

irreconcilable differences, an inability to agree or solve problems together, leading to the breakdown of a relationship. See NO-FAULT DIVORCE, GROUNDS FOR DIVORCE.

issue. See OFFSPRING.

"I" statements, a communication technique in which the speaker addresses problems by beginning sentences with the word "I" in order to focus on his or her own feelings and opinions rather than appearing to blame the other person by starting with "you".

it takes two to tango, *proverb*. Both parties involved in a situation or problem bear responsibility. Popularized by a 1952 song written by Al Hoffman and Dick Manning.

J

jealousy, *n.* 1. resentment against a rival, or against someone who has greater success or advantages. 2. feelings of fear, anxiety, insecurity, and pain over the loss or anticipated loss to a rival of something of great personal value, particularly in connection with an important relationship.

Jeeves, *n.* the personification of the perfect valet or butler. Jeeves is the name of a character in a series of stories and novels by P.G. Wodehouse.

Jocasta complex, *psych.* the obsessive attachment of a mother to her son. In Greek mythology, Jocasta unwittingly married her son, Oedipus. The term was introduced by Raymond de Saussure in the 1920s.

Johnny-come-lately, *idiom.* a newcomer.

Johnson, Sue. clinical psychologist, researcher, and professor, the primary developer of Emotionally Focused Therapy. Johnson's work has widely influenced the couples counseling movement.

joined at the hip, *idiom.* inseparable; very closely connected, rarely or never going anywhere without each other.

journeyman, *n.* a worker who has advanced beyond apprenticeship; a reliable worker.

Judas, *n.* a treacherous person who betrays a friend. From the Biblical account of Judas Iscariot, a disciple who betrayed Jesus. See KISS OF DEATH.

jump down [someone]'s throat, *idiom.* quickly or suddenly respond by harshly criticizing someone.

jumping the broom, *idiom.* getting married. Derived from "broomstick marriage," an 18th century expression used to describe a marriage of doubtful validity. In the U.S. during the 19th century, a wedding ceremony in which the bride and groom jumped over a broomstick was sometimes used by slaves, who were often denied access to legal marriage and therefore created their own rituals.

jump/climb on the bandwagon, *idiom.* 1. join a popular movement or activity. 2. go along with what everyone else is doing.

Historically, a bandwagon was a horse-drawn platform that carried a loud musical group promoting a political candidate. People who wanted to show support for the candidate would climb aboard.

K

keep company, 1. spend time together. 2. date.

keep [someone] at arm's length, *idiom.* 1. avoid familiarity with someone. 2. prevent someone from getting involved or gaining information.

keep up with the Joneses, *idiom.* attempt to match the lifestyle of one's neighbors in order to maintain equal status with them. This term was popularized by a cartoon strip during the first part of the 20th century.

kibitz, *v. Yiddish.* interfere or give unwanted advice while others are busy, especially at a card game.

kick [someone/something] to the curb, *idiom.* 1. expel someone from a particular location. 2. end a relationship with someone. 3. dismiss someone or something in a summary manner. Possibly derived from the practice of setting trash out at the curb.

kid, *n.* 1. a young goat. 2. a child or young person. *v.* 3. tease or be deceptive as a joke.

kidnap, *v.* illegally take or detain a person by force or fraud.

kin, kinfolk, *n.* one's relatives.

kindred, *n.* 1. a group of related people. *adj.* 2. having the same feelings, beliefs, or attitudes. 3. connected by kinship.

kindred spirit, someone whose beliefs, attitudes, or feelings are very similar to one's own.

Kinsey Reports, two published studies, *Sexual Behavior in the Human Male* (1948) and *Sexual Behavior in the Human Female* (1953), authored by Alfred Kinsey, Wardell Pomeroy, et al. The reports, intended to provide a large body of quantifiable data on sexual behavior, were based on interviews with thousands of subjects.

kinship, *n.* family relationship or consanguinity.

kinsman, kinswoman, *n.* a relative.

kiss, *v.* 1. touch with one's lips as a sign of greeting, affection, respect, love, or sexual interest. 2. join lips. *n.* 3. the act of touching with the lips or joining lips.

kiss a frog, kissing a frog, *idiom.* based on an old folk tale about a princess who reluctantly kisses a frog, who then is released from an evil spell and restored to his identity as a prince. Often used to express the idea that a good romantic partner may not appear attractive at first, or, more cynically, that most frogs are just frogs and not princes.

kissing cousins, *idiom.* 1. a relative, such as a second (or more distant) cousin with whom it would be socially acceptable to have a romantic relationship or marriage. 2. *rare.* a relative one knows well enough to greet with a kiss.

kiss of death, *idiom.* 1. an action which proves destructive or fatal to an endeavor or a relationship. 2. a kiss or symbolic gesture given to someone who is about to be dismissed, betrayed, or killed. 3. betrayal disguised as a friendly gesture. Also called a **Judas kiss,** from the Biblical story of Judas, who kissed Jesus in order to betray him.

kiss off, *idiom.* 1. reject. 2. **kiss-off,** an act of rejection or dismissal.

kiss up, *idiom.* curry favor.

kith, *n.* friends, acquaintances, and neighbors. Commonly used in the phrase "kith and kin," meaning all of one's acquaintances and relatives.

knight in shining armor, *idiom.* a person who helps or saves someone from a difficult or dangerous situation, especially a man rescuing a woman. Derived from the idealized concept of a chivalrous knight of the Middle Ages.

know [someone] like a book, *idiom.* have a complete understanding of someone.

kowtow, *v.* 1. kneel with the forehead touching the ground as an act of worship or submission, especially as part of a Chinese custom. 2. behave in an overly obsequious manner.

lackey, *n*. 1. a servant who wears a uniform. 2. a toady.

ladies' man, a man who expends much time and energy attracting and flirting with women.

lady in waiting, a personal assistant to a queen, princess, or high-ranking noblewoman.

lady-killer, *idiom*. an attractive man who is irresistible to women.

lady of the house, the female head of household.

landlord (*masc.* or *fem.*), **landlady** (*fem.*), *n*. someone who owns or manages, and leases to others, apartments, houses, buildings, or land.

lap dog, 1. a small pet dog. 2. a person who is controlled by another.

laughing stock, a person who is an object of ridicule.

lead by the nose, *idiom*. dominate or control someone. From the practice of putting rings through the noses of cattle in order to lead them.

lead [someone] on, *idiom*. intentionally mislead someone.

leader, *n*. 1. someone who precedes others physically or in sequence. 2. someone who guides, directs, or commands a group, organization, or government. 3. a person who holds a dominant or superior position in a field of endeavor; someone who is recognized for outstanding ability. 4. someone who has great influence. 5. someone who inspires or motivates others. 6. the principal player in a musical group.

leadership, *n*. 1. the position or condition of being a leader. 2. the action of guiding or directing a group or organization. 3. the group of leaders within an organization.

leadership style, the behavior, attitudes, and methods of someone in a position of leadership. In the 1930s, psychologist Karl Lewin identified three main leadership styles: authoritarian, democratic, and laissez-faire. Subsequent studies have identified many additional styles and patterns of leadership.

Leap Day, February 29th, a date that occurs only in leap years. In some places, folk tradition designates this as a day for women to propose marriage.

leave [someone] alone, 1. leave someone in solitude. 2. refrain from bothering or interacting with someone.

leer, *v.* look at someone in a malicious or lecherous manner.

legal separation, 1. in some states, a legally specified period of time during which a couple must live apart before they can divorce. 2. in other states, legal separation occurs when a married couple lives apart without divorcing, but undergoes a court procedure similar to divorce in which the division of property, child custody, and other terms and conditions are determined. In some jurisdictions, this kind of legal separation is known as a limited divorce. See DIVORCE.

lesbian, *n.* a homosexual woman.

levirate marriage, a custom whereby a deceased man's brother is obligated to marry his widow. This practice appears in various religious and cultural traditions. It purpose may be to protect a widow and her children, to ensure inheritance, or to solidify family ties. See SORORATE MARRIAGE.

liaison, *n.* 1. a connection maintained between military units or sections of an organization in order to ensure cooperation and coordinated action. 2. a person responsible for such a connection. 3. an intimate, illicit meeting or relationship.

lie, *n.* 1. an intentionally false or misleading statement. *v.* 2. make a false statement.

life coach, a person who encourages and counsels clients on understanding and improving their careers, relationships, and goals.

life of the party, *idiom.* a person whose energy and charm enliven a social occasion.

life partner, one member of a long-term, monogamous relationship.

like, *v.* 1. enjoy or find pleasant. 2. feel friendly toward. 3. view in a positive way. 4. *coll.* on social media, to click a symbol on someone's post or picture as a way of indicating a positive or supportive response.

limerence, *n.* an intense, overwhelming state of infatuation and romantic obsession. Coined in the 1970s by Dorothy Tennov. Rarely used now.

little black book, *idiom.* a small address book in which someone writes contact information, especially phone numbers of past or potential lovers. Today this has been largely replaced by electronic devices.

little woman, the, *idiom.* one's wife. Facetious, often considered demeaning.

living apart together, *idiom.* an arrangement in which a married couple or a couple in a long-term, committed relationship maintains separate residences. Sometimes abbreviated LAT.

lonely, *adj.* 1. sad because of an absence of companionship. 2. alone. 3. characterized by solitude.

loner, *n.* a person who spends a great deal of time alone and avoids the company of others.

lonesome, *adj.* 1. sad because of an absence of companionship. 2. characterized by solitude.

lone wolf, a loner; someone who prefers to work or act alone.

long distance relationship, a friendship, romance, or association in which the participants live far apart from each other.

long lost, *idiom.* not seen or contacted for a long time.

long time no see, *idiom.* a greeting used by people who have not seen each other in a long time.

look after, pay attention to or take care of.

look daggers at, *idiom.* stare at someone in an angry or threatening way.

look down on [someone], *idiom.* feel superior to someone; view someone with contempt. Also, **look down one's nose** at someone.

look in on, visit someone.

look out for [someone], 1. behave protectively toward someone. 2. be on guard against someone.

look [someone] up, *idiom.* locate someone, or find someone's contact information.

look up to [someone], *idiom.* admire someone.

loose cannon, *idiom.* a person whose unpredictable behavior is likely to cause trouble. Derived from a description in Victor Hugo's 1874 novel *Ninety-Three*, in which an unsecured cannon rolled around dangerously on the deck of a warship.

lose face. See FACE.

lose one's heart, *idiom.* fall in love. (However, to **lose heart** is to become discouraged.)

loss of consortium, a legal claim made against a defendant whose actions have caused injury to the plaintiff's spouse, resulting in a loss of normal marital relations.

Lothario, *n.* a man who habitually seduces and deceives women. From a character in the 1703 play *The Fair Penitent* by Nicholas Rowe.

love, *n.* 1. an intense feeling of affection and personal connection. 2. a feeling of deep romantic or sexual attachment. 3. a strong feeling of liking, pleasure, and interest in something. 4. affectionate concern for the well-being of others. 5. a person toward whom one has feelings of romantic love. 6. a term of endearment. 7. a personification of sexual or romantic love, such as Cupid. *v.* 8. have strong feelings of affection. 9. feel a deep romantic or sexual attachment. 10. have a strong liking or enjoyment of something.

love affair, 1. a romantic or sexual relationship. 2. an ongoing enthusiasm for something.

love at first sight, the development of affection and emotional attachment upon meeting someone for the first time; a sudden infatuation.

lovebirds, *n. pl. idiom.* a couple that displays a great deal of affection. Derived from the name of small pet birds known for their displays of affection.

love child, *archaic*. a child born to unmarried parents.

loved one, a highly valued family member or friend.

love-hate relationship, a relationship characterized by alternating or simultaneous feelings of love and hate.

love is blind, *proverb*. People don't see the flaws in those they love. First appeared in Chaucer's "Merchant's Tale" (c. 1045), popularized by Shakespeare's "Merchant of Venice" (1596).

love languages, a theory introduced by Gary Chapman, which proposes that people have five basic ways of expressing and receiving love (words of affirmation, quality time, gifts, acts of service, and physical touch), and that individuals tend to be strongly oriented to only one or two of these.

lovelorn, *adj*. feeling sad and lonely as a result of unrequited love.

love match, a marriage or relationship based solely or primarily on love and affection.

love nest, *idiom*. an apartment or room where lovers meet, often clandestinely.

love potion, a supposedly magical or medicinal concoction believed to arouse love or sexual desire.

lover, *n*. 1. someone who is in love. 2. someone involved in an amorous relationship. 3. someone involved in an illicit affair; a paramour. 4. a person who has a very strong liking for something. 5. a person who shows great affection for others.

lovers' lane, a secluded path or road used by lovers seeking privacy.

lovers' leap, a cliff or peak where lovelorn people jump to their deaths.

love seat, a small sofa or bench designed for two people.

lovesick, *adj*. feeling miserable or ill as a result of unrequited love; lovelorn.

love triangle, *idiom*. a situation in which one person is involved in romantic relationships with two others.

lovey dovey, *idiom.* as a couple, behaving in a highly affectionate manner.

low man on the totem pole, *idiom.* the least important person in an organization or group. Based on the incorrect assumption that figures carved at the bottom of a totem pole are less important than others.

loyal, *adj.* 1. faithfully devoted to a person, group, country, or idea. 2. reliably committed to one's promises, obligations, and duties.

lust, *n.* 1. sexual appetite. 2. excessive or inappropriate sexual desire. 3. powerful enthusiasm.

M

madam, *n.* 1. a courtesy title for a woman, especially one in a position of authority. Often shortened to **ma'am**. 2. a female pimp.

magnetic personality, a personality that is highly appealing to others.

maiden name, a woman's surname at birth. See MARRIED NAME.

maid of honor. See BRIDESMAID.

mail order bride, a woman who advertises herself (whether in a printed catalog, newspaper, or website) with the intention of finding a husband.

    Historically, men who migrated to the western frontier of North America in the 19th century found themselves in areas where few women lived. They conducted courtships by writing letters to women they contacted through personal advertisements. Today, the term is associated primarily with women in Eastern Europe or Asia who wish to marry men in other countries.

main squeeze, *slang.* The person with whom one has one's primary romantic relationship.

maître d' (shortened form of maître d'hôtel), *n.* at a restaurant, the person who handles reservations and supervises the waitstaff. French, "master of [the] hotel".

majordomo, *n.* the chief steward or head servant of a large household.

majority, *n.* the age at which a person is legally considered to be an adult.

make an honest woman of her, *idiom.* marry a woman subsequent to having sexual relations. Based on an old-fashioned notion of protecting or restoring her reputation or chastity. Now used facetiously.

make a pass at, *idiom.* attempt to get a physically affectionate or sexual response from someone.

make eyes at, *idiom.* gaze at someone flirtatiously.

make fun of, mock or belittle.

make it up to [someone], *idiom*. attempt to compensate someone for a disappointment or loss.

make love, 1. engage in sexual intercourse. 2. embrace and kiss passionately. 3. *obs.* declare one's amorous feelings and intentions to someone.

make out, *coll.* 1. get a result or achieve a goal: "How did you make out at the interview?" 2. embrace and kiss passionately.

make [someone]'s acquaintance. meet someone for the first time.

make up, *v.* 1. reconcile after an argument. 2. compensate for a failure or loss.

make up to [someone], *idiom*. try to become friendly with someone.

malign, *v.* slander or defame someone.

mama, mamma, momma, mommie, mommy, nicknames for mother.

mama's boy, 1. a man who is overly attached to his mother at an age when he is expected to be independent. 2. a boy or young man who is overly controlled or protected by his mother. See DADDY'S GIRL.

man Friday, girl Friday, *idiom*. a personal assistant. From the character Friday in the 1719 novel *Robinson Crusoe* by Daniel Defoe.

manner, *n.* 1. a way of doing something. 2. a person's outward bearing and social behavior.

manners, *n.* 1. polite standards of behavior. 2. the customary ways of behaving and living.

man of the house, the male head of household.

man's best friend, *idiom*. the dog. Possibly originated in the 1820s.

manservant, *n.* a male servant.

man's man, a man who gets along well with other men and who is characterized by his involvement in traditionally masculine activities.

marital, *adj*. having to do with marriage.

marital assets, marital property, all the money and property belonging to a married couple.

marital status, the state of being single, married, widowed, separated, or divorced.

marital therapy. See COUPLES COUNSELING.

marriage, *n*. a socially or legally recognized contract between spouses that establishes the rights and obligations they have with each other and any children they may produce, and sometimes with their respective families. Marriage is considered a "cultural universal" because some form of marriage exists in all cultures. It is recognized variously as a legal, religious, or social institution. See DIVORCE, WEDDING.

marriage bed, 1. the bed in which a married couple sleeps. 2. the sexual relationship between a married couple.

marriage by proxy, a wedding in which one or both spouses are not physically present. Proxy marriages are legally recognized in only a few places, and are generally subject to many restrictions.

marriage ceremony, the act of formally uniting a couple in marriage. See WEDDING.

marriage certificate, 1. an official document indicating that a marriage has been legally registered. 2. a document provided by a clergyperson or officiant to show that a marriage ceremony took place.

marriage counselor, marriage counseling. See COUPLES COUNSELING.

marriage license, a document issued by a governing agency that grants permission for a couple to marry. Receiving a license does not mean that the couple is married. They still must undergo a ceremony (before the license expires) and register the marriage. Requirements and regulations vary by jurisdiction.

marriage made in heaven, *idiom*. a perfect marriage, seemingly predestined.

marriage of convenience, a marriage motivated primarily by reasons other than the relationship or family. People sometimes marry in order to gain political, social, or financial advantages. In most cases there is nothing illegal or illicit about such a marriage, as long as both parties consent. However, some marriages of convenience are considered fraudulent, as when an immigrant marries a citizen for the sole purpose of gaining residency status.

marriage proposal, the act of asking someone to marry.

marriage registration, 1. an official record of a marriage. 2. the act of recording a marriage with a governing agency. In the past, marriages were often recorded only in church records or in family documents. Today, most jurisdictions require that marriages be recorded at a central location, such as a county or state office. Marriages not officially recorded may not be considered legally valid.

married name, a name taken by someone upon marriage, especially when a woman assumes her husband's surname. Although women in the U.S. are often under social pressure to change their names, there is no legal requirement to do so. Some women choose to keep their own names; others hyphenate their name with their spouse's name. Sometimes both partners hyphenate, infrequently a man takes his spouse's name, and in rare cases couples choose a new name for the marriage. There are some countries where both men and women are legally required to keep their birth names, although married names may be used socially. In many countries, a name change upon marriage is simply not part of the culture.

marry, *v.* 1. take someone as husband or wife. 2. unite a couple in marriage by performing a wedding ceremony. 3. **marry off**, find a spouse for someone, especially a family member, sometimes said with the implication of relief at getting a child out of the parental home.

marry in haste, repent at leisure, *proverb*. People who rush into marriage will have the rest of their lives to regret it. Originated in the 1500s.

marry up, **marry down**. See HYPERGAMY and HYPOGAMY.

martinet, *n.* a strict disciplinarian.

masher, *n. archaic*. a man who makes unwanted advances to women.

mass hysteria, irrational behavior and beliefs, or symptoms of illness, that spread rapidly through a group of people, based on rumors, fear, and suggestibility.

mass wedding. See COLLECTIVE WEDDING.

master, *n*. 1. someone who has great power and proficiency in an area of skill, art, or knowledge. 2. the owner of an animal or a slave. 3. the male head of a household. 4. the captain of a merchant vessel. 5. a victor or conqueror. 6. someone who has received a master's degree. 7. someone who is in charge of servants or other workers. 8. someone who has been entrusted with specific responsibilities and authority over a task or activity.

Master, *archaic*. courtesy title for boys or young, unmarried men.

Masters and Johnson, William H. Masters (1915-2001) and Virginia E. Johnson (1925-2013), researchers noted for their studies of human sexuality and publication of the book *Human Sexual Response* (1966).

matchmaker, *n*. a person who attempts to arrange marriages by finding and introducing potential mates.

mate, *n*. 1. one of a pair. 2. a spouse. 3. a comrade or fellow worker. *v*. in reference to animals, to form a pair bond or engage in sexual activity.

-mate, suffix indicating that two people share the same space or are involved in the same activity: classmate, roommate.

maternal, *adj*. having to do with mothers or mothering.

maternal instinct, a mother's natural impulse to love and protect her child.

matriarch, *n*. the female head of a family, clan, or tribe.

matrilineal, *adj*. determining inheritance or descent through the female line.

matrilocal, *adj. anth*. pertaining to the residence of one's wife's family or tribe.

matrilocality, *n. anth*. a custom or social system whereby a married couple lives with or near the wife's family.

matrimonial, *adj*. relating to marriage.

matrimony, *n*. marriage.

matron of honor. See BRIDESMAID.

May-December romance, *idiom.* a romance between two people who are very far apart in age. Sometimes called a **May-September** relationship or an **age-gap** relationship.

Medea complex, *psych.* the desire of a mother to kill her children, particularly as a means of revenge against her husband. In Greek mythology, Medea killed her children after their father, Jason, left her for another woman.

medium. See SÉANCE.

meet cute, *idiom.* a scene in a film or TV show in which a couple meets for the first time in a way that is considered amusing or especially appealing, especially if the circumstances are unusual or comical.

meeting, *n.* 1. an encounter between two or more people. 2. a gathering of people for a particular purpose.

ménage à trois, *French.* 1. a domestic arrangement in which a married couple and the lover of one (or both) of them live together. 2. a sexual encounter involving three people.

mend fences, *idiom.* reconcile or make peace after a disagreement.

mentor, *n.* an experienced and trusted adviser. In *The Odyssey*, Mentor was the name of a loyal friend who was entrusted with the care and education of Odysseus's son Telemachus.

middleman, *n.* an intermediary between two parties in a business transaction.

midwife, *n.* a person (traditionally a woman) who assists women in childbirth.

minder, *n.* 1. a person who takes care of or watches over something or someone. 2. a person employed to escort and guide another, often with the aim of providing protection or monitoring behavior.

mind games, psychological manipulation intended to confuse, mislead, or intimidate another, especially for the purpose of gaining an advantage.

mind reading, 1. the supposed ability to know another's thoughts through extrasensory methods. 2. assuming or imagining that one knows others' thoughts and motives, especially for the purpose of criticizing them.

minimax principle. See SOCIAL EXCHANGE THEORY.

minion, *n*. 1. a follower or subordinate of someone in power. 2. a minor official. 3. **minion of the law**, police officer.

minor, *n*. 1. a child; someone who is not legally an adult. 2. a person who is below the age of consent.

mirroring, *n. psych.* 1. behavior in which one person unconsciously imitates the posture, gestures, or speech patterns of another. 2. intentionally imitating another's movements or speech for the purpose of building rapport.

mirror neuron, a kind of brain cell that reacts equally when one performs an action and when one observes another performing the same action. Scientists believe that mirror neurons allow us to understand and interpret other people's intentions and facial expressions, thus playing a significant role in our ability to feel empathy, predict behavior, and socialize with others.

misally, *v.* form a poorly-chosen alliance.

misandry, *n.* hatred of men.

misanthropy, *n.* hatred of people in general. A person who lives a life of misanthropy is a **misanthrope**.

miscegenation, *n. obs.* marriage, cohabitation, or interbreeding between persons of different races.

misery loves company, *proverb.* 1. It is easier to bear suffering if you are not alone. 2. Unhappy people like to make other people unhappy.

misogamy, *n.* hatred of marriage.

misogyny, *n.* hatred of women.

Miss, a courtesy title for girls or unmarried women.

Mister, a courtesy title for men, usually abbreviated as Mr.

mistress, *n*. 1. a woman in a position of power and authority, especially regarding a household or domestic workers. 2. the female owner of an animal or slave. 3. a woman who has an ongoing affair with a married man, especially one who provides her with gifts or financial support. 4. *archaic*. a courtesy title for a woman.

mistrust, *n*. 1. lack of trust; distrust. *v*. 2. be distrustful or suspicious of someone.

mixed marriage, a marriage between people of different races or religions.

mollify, *v*. pacify or soothe someone's anger or anxiety.

mom, *n*. *inf*. mother.

mommie, mommy, momma, nicknames for mother.

Mommie Dearest, *idiom*. a domineering, emotionally abusive mother. Popularized in the 1980s by the book and movie based on Christina Crawford's memories of her mother, Joan.

monogamy, *n*. the practice of having only one mate at a time. Sociologists, anthropologists, and biologists often break this into several categories. **Social monogamy** refers to a pair's social and living arrangement. They are partners in life, but may or may not have a sexual (or sexually exclusive) relationship. **Sexual monogamy** refers to sexual exclusivity. **Genetic monogamy** means that DNA analysis of offspring confirms that a male-female pair mate exclusively with each other. The term **strict monogamy** is sometimes used to mean having only one mate for life. **Serial monogamy** refers to a succession of monogamous relationships (married or otherwise). Usually this implies sexual exclusivity for the duration of each relationship.

more space, *idiom*. In the context of a romantic relationship, the phrase "I need more space" often indicates a desire for less involvement in the relationship. **Space** may also refer to privacy or a need for temporary solitude in order to work or relax.

morganatic marriage, a marriage between a man of high rank, typically a member of a royal family, and a lower-ranking woman, in which the wife and any children produced by the marriage are not allowed to inherit the husband's title and property.

mother, *n*. 1. a female parent. *v*. 2. care for someone in a maternal way or as a mother.

motherese. See BABY TALK.

mother figure, 1. a woman who appears to embody the characteristics of an idealized mother. 2. a female relative or friend who provides a role model for a child, especially one whose mother is dead or absent. 3. a father or male caretaker who attempts to fill a missing mother's role.

motherhood, *n*. the state of being a mother.

mother-in-law, *pl*. mothers-in-law. *n*. the mother of one's spouse.

Mother's Day, a holiday established to honor mothers, celebrated in the U.S. on the second Sunday of May.

mother's helper, a person (traditionally a young woman) hired to help with household chores and child care.

mother superior, the head of a female religious community.

mourn, *v*. feel or express sorrow and grief for someone or something that is gone, especially for someone who has died.

mourner, *n*. 1. someone who attends a funeral as a relative or friend of the deceased. 2. **professional mourner**, someone who is paid to attend a funeral and appear to grieve.

mouth to feed, another, *idiom*. a child, pet, or other dependent who is provided with food or other necessities.

move in the same circles, *idiom*. associate with the same groups of people.

Mr., pl. Messrs. *abbr*. Mister, a courtesy title for men.

Mr. Right, Ms. Right, Miss Right, a hypothetical perfect future spouse.

Mrs., *abbr*. a courtesy title for a married woman or widow, particularly one who uses her husband's surname. Originally an abbreviation for "mistress," it is now pronounced "MISS-uz" and occasionally spelled out, informally, as "Missus" .

Ms., a courtesy title for women, pronounced "miz". It first appeared in print around 1949 as a blend of "Miss" and "Mrs." It gained popularity beginning in the 1970s as a female equivalent of "Mr.", which does not reveal marital status. However, when marital status is known, many people still use "Mrs." for married women and "Ms." for the unmarried.

multiples, *n. pl.* Two or more children born together. Two are twins, three are triplets, four are quadruplets, five are quintuplets, six are sextuplets, seven are septuplets, and eight are octuplets. There are a few documented cases of nonuplets being born, but none who survived more than a few hours. Advancements in the medical treatment of infertility have led to an increase in the number of multiples born. See TWINS.

murder. See HOMICIDE.

muse, *n.* 1. a person who provides ongoing inspiration for a writer, composer, painter, or other artist. 2. in classical mythology, the Muses were nine sister goddesses who presided over the arts.

nag, *v.* 1. complain in a persistent, irritating manner. *n.* 2. a person who constantly complains and makes persistent, irritating demands.

name, *n.* 1. a word or words used to identify or refer to a specific person, animal, place, or thing. 2. one's reputation. 3. a prominent person: "He was a big name." 4. a designation not supported by facts: "He was the boss in name only." 5. a derogatory appellation: "She called him names." *v.* 6. give someone or something a name. 7. appoint: "I have named him the new chief." 8. identify or accuse.

name-calling, *idiom.* the use of insulting words toward someone.

name-dropping, *idiom.* attempting to impress others by referring to one's relationships with prominent people.

nanny, *n.* a child's nursemaid or caretaker.

neck, *v. slang. archaic.* embrace and kiss passionately.

neglect, *v.* 1. ignore or pay little attention to. 2. fail to provide proper care for someone or something. 3. fail to carry out one's duties or obligations. *n.* 4. the act or ongoing behavior of neglecting. 5. the condition of having been neglected.

neighbor, *n.* 1. a person who lives near another. 2. a person who is standing or sitting next to someone. 3. a fellow human being.

neighborhood, *n.* 1. the region surrounding a particular place or thing. 2. a district or locality, often in reference to its special characteristics. 3. a group of people who live near each other.

nemesis, *n.* 1. a person or force that brings retribution. 2. an unconquerable opponent or rival. 3. In classical mythology, Nemesis was the goddess of divine retribution.

neonate, *n.* a newborn child.

nepotism, *n.* patronage or favoritism in business or politics, based on family relationships. Derived from the Latin *nepos* (nephew or grandson).

network, *v.* meet and converse with people, especially at meetings or events, for the purpose of cultivating those who may be helpful in one's profession. See SOCIAL NETWORK.

new kid on the block, *idiom.* a newcomer, especially one who is young or inexperienced.

newlywed, *n.* a recently married person. Traditionally, people are considered newlyweds during the first year of marriage.

nickname, *n.* 1. a modified, less formal version of one's given name. 2. a name or word substituted for one's actual name. Nicknames are often used familiarly and affectionately among friends and relatives, but are also sometimes used as a means of ridicule.

nodding acquaintance, a person one knows slightly, just enough to recognize and greet or nod to in passing.

no-fault divorce, a divorce that does not require one party to prove fault on the part of the other. The initiating party only needs to state the reason for the divorce (typically "irreconcilable differences"). See DIVORCE and GROUNDS FOR DIVORCE.

no love lost between them, *idiom.* They don't like each other.

nonconsensual, *adj.* not agreed to by one or more of the people involved.

noncustodial, *adj.* not having custody of one's children.

normative social influence, *psych.* the influence of other people that leads one to adapt one's behavior to conform with a group; peer pressure.

nosy, *adj.* overly inquisitive.

nuclear family. See FAMILY.

nuptial, *adj.* pertaining to marriage.

nuptials, *n.* a wedding ceremony.

nurse, *n.* 1. someone who has been educated and trained to care for the sick and infirm, and to provide health care services. *v.* 2. provide care to a sick or infirm person or animal. 3. breastfeed a baby.

nursemaid, a servant who takes care of children.

nurture, *v.* 1. provide nourishment and support for the growth and development of a child or other living organism. 2. provide support and assistance to promote someone's development, maturation, or success.

O

obedience, *n.* compliance.

obey, *v.* 1. comply with a command or request. 2. behave in accordance with a principle, instinct, feeling, natural law, etc.

objectify, *v.* treat someone as an object rather than a person.

obsequious, *adj.* servile or deferential to an extreme degree.

odd couple, *idiom.* a seemingly mismatched couple.

odd man out, *idiom.* a person who is isolated from the group, or one who does not fit in.

Oedipus complex, a psychological theory, introduced by Sigmund Freud, that children go through a stage of development in which they feel a sense of rivalry with the same-sex parent while desiring sexual relations with the opposite sex parent. In females, this is often called an Electra complex. Derived from a story in Greek mythology, in which Oedipus unwittingly killed his father and married his mother. In another story, Electra plotted with her brother Orestes to kill their mother as revenge for the murder of their father.

office politics, the strategies and influences used by people in the workplace to gain advantages for themselves or the policies they support.

offspring, *n.* 1. one's child or children. Sometimes referred to as **issue** in a legal or genealogical context. 2. descendants.

ogle, *v.* stare in a lecherous manner.

old boy network, *idiom.* social and business connections whereby influential men assist each other, often as alumni of the same school or members of private clubs, typically to the exclusion of women and ethnic minorities.

old flame, *idiom.* 1. a former lover or person with whom one had a romantic relationship in the past. 2. a person one was attracted to or had romantic feelings for in the past.

old lady, *slang*. 1. one's mother. 2. one's wife. Sometimes considered mildly derogatory.

old maid, *idiom. archaic*. derogatory term for a woman who has remained unmarried beyond the usual age for marriage.

old man, *slang*. 1. one's father. 2. one's husband. Sometimes considered mildly derogatory.

ombudsman, *n.* an official appointed to investigate individuals' complaints against government agencies or corporations.

one, the, *idiom*. An idealized concept of one's future mate, sometimes thought to be predestined. See SOULMATE.

one night stand, *idiom*. 1. a sexual relationship that lasts only one night. 2. a single performance of a play or show in a particular location.

one-sided relationship, 1. a relationship in which one person invests significantly more effort or emotion than the other. 2. a relationship which is of interest to only one of the parties.

one-upmanship, *n.* the practice of achieving superiority over a friend or rival, often in petty ways.

online dating, the practice of looking for a potential romantic or sexual partner via specialized websites.

only child, a child without siblings.

on speaking terms, *idiom*. 1. casually acquainted with someone. 2. willing to converse with someone. 2. **not on speaking terms**, refusing to speak with someone because of a disagreement.

on the outs, *idiom*. not on good terms with someone.

on the rocks, *idiom*. in reference to a relationship: on the verge of breaking up. Derived from the disastrous situation of a ship crashing on rocks near the seashore.

open marriage. See POLYGAMY.

opponent, *n.* adversary.

opposite number, someone who holds an equivalent or similar job or position in a different system, company, or country.

opposites attract, *proverb*. Dissimilar people are often drawn to each other.

opsigamy, *n. rare.* marriage when old.

orphan, *n.* a child whose parents have died.

ostracize, *v.* exclude someone, by mutual consent, from a social group or from society in general.

outgroup, *n. soc.* people outside of one's own group, viewed as inferior or in opposition.

out of [one's] league, *idiom.* a desired romantic partner's attractiveness or personal characteristics are greatly superior to one's own. Derived from the system of major and minor leagues in sports.

out of sight, out of mind, *proverb*. When people are apart, they don't often think of each other. Possibly originated with John Heywood in 1562.

out of wedlock, outside of marriage. Often used in reference to the birth of a child.

oxytocin, *n.* a hormone sometimes nicknamed the "love hormone" because of its association with physical contact and social bonding.

P

pair, *n*. 1. two identical, similar, or matched items that are used together: a pair of shoes. 2. two people or animals that are associated in some way. 3. a married, engaged, or dating couple. 4. two mated animals. *v*. 5. match or connect two items, animals, or people. 6. bring two animals together for the purpose of mating.

pair bond, a close attachment formed through courtship and sexual activity.

pair off or **pair up**, 1. form pairs for an activity, such as dancing. 2. form a close partnership, as in business or marriage.

pal, *n*. a comrade or chum.

palimony, *n*. a division of property or alimony-like support paid to a former unmarried partner. The word was coined in the 1970s, probably by Marvin Mitchelson, by combining "pal" with "alimony".

papa, pop, poppa, pappy, nicknames for father.

paramour, *n*. *archaic*. an illicit lover, especially of a married person.

parasite, *n*. 1. someone who receives financial support, long-term hospitality, or other advantages from others without giving anything in return. 2. In biology: an organism that lives on or in another and derives nutrients at the host's expense.

pard, pardner, *n*. *coll.* partner.

parent, *n*. 1. a mother, father, stepmother or stepfather. *v*. 2. be a parent or care for someone like a parent.

parental investment, *biol.* any resources (such as time and energy) expended by a parent for the benefit of one offspring, which carries a cost, including the cost of limiting the parent's ability to produce additional offspring.

parenting marriage, an arrangement in which a married couple lives in the same household, cooperatively and amicably, for the purpose of being with and caring for their children. They do not have a romantic or sexual relationship with each other, but may be free to do so with others.

pariah, *n.* an outcast; one who is despised.

part company, 1. go different ways; separate. 2. end an association. 3. assume a different opinion from someone else.

partible paternity, *anth.* the belief that a child can have more than one biological father.

partner, *n.* 1. a person who shares or is associated with another in some endeavor. 2. a co-owner or co-investor in a business. 3. someone who is assigned to work with another. 4. a spouse. 5. someone who cohabits with another. 6. a person who engages with another in an activity such as dancing or tennis.

partnership, *n.* 1. the relationship between partners; the state of being a partner. 2. a business operated by partners.

partners in crime, 1. people who commit crimes together. 2. *idiom.* good friends who have adventures or get into mischief together.

party, *n.* 1. a social gathering of invited guests. 2. a group brought together for a special purpose, such as a search party. 3. a group of persons organized around common political ideas. 4. one of the participants in an activity, contract, lawsuit, or crime. 5. one or more persons attending a restaurant, social function, or cultural event. *v. coll.* 6. have fun at a party or event. 7. behave in a highly celebratory manner, especially under the influence of alcohol.

party animal, *slang.* a highly gregarious person who enjoys parties, especially one who indulges in alcohol and wild behavior.

party crasher, someone who attends a party without having been invited, especially one who causes problems or behaves offensively.

party pooper, *slang.* a negative or unpleasant person whose presence reduces others' enjoyment of an event.

passing fancy, a temporary interest or enthusiasm.

pass the buck, *idiom.* avoid responsibility by passing it to someone else.

paterfamilias, *n.* the male head of a household, especially the father.

paternal, *adj.* having to do with fathers or fatherhood.

paternal instinct, a father's natural impulse to love and protect his child.

paternity, *n.* fatherhood.

paternity suit, a court case for the purpose of formally establishing the identity of a child's father.

patient, *n.* a person who receives treatment from a doctor or other medical practitioner.

patriarch, *n.* 1. the male head of a family, clan or tribe. 2. a man who is regarded as a founder of an ancestral line, religious order, nation, etc. 3. a man who is the oldest and most respected leader or member of a group. 4. one of the early Biblical personages regarded as founders of the human race. 5. one of the Biblical personages regarded as the progenitors of the Israelites or the tribes of Israel.

patrilineal, *adj.* inheritance or ancestry determined through the male line.

patrilocal, *adj. anth.* pertaining to the residence of one's husband's family or tribe.

patrilocality, *n. anth.* a custom or social system whereby a married couple lives with or near the husband's family.

patron, *n.* 1. a customer, client, or paying guest. 2. a person who provides material or financial support or endorsements for an organization, cause, or individual.

pay back, *v.* 1. return borrowed money. 2. return a favor. 3. get revenge.

payback, *n.* 1. revenge. 2. payment of a debt. 3. return on an investment.

peace offering, a gift offered as a gesture of conciliation.

pedophilia, *n.* 1. a sexual interest in young children. 2. the act of sexually molesting young children. A person who sexually molests children is a **pedophile**.

pedophobia, *n.* fear of children.

peer, *n.* 1. someone who has equal social or legal rank. 2. someone whose abilities are equal. 3. in Great Britain, a nobleman.

peer group, 1. a social group with which one identifies and associates. 2. a social group of people who are similar in age and status.

peer marriage. See EGALITARIAN MARRIAGE.

peer pressure, strong influence from one's peers or social group, especially during adolescence.

Penelope, *n.* in Greek mythology, the wife of Odysseus. While her husband was away for ten years, she waited for him, refusing many eager suitors. Sometimes used as a synonym for a faithful wife.

pen pal, a person with whom one has a relationship based primarily or solely on an exchange of correspondence.

people pleaser, *idiom.* someone who feels compelled to help and care for others to an excessive degree, often neglecting his or her own needs.

people watching, lingering in a public place for the purpose of observing other people as a relaxing pastime.

person, *pl.* people, persons. *n.* an individual human being.

personal assistant, an employee who works closely with an individual (typically a business executive), helping to manage that person's daily schedule and tasks.

personal boundaries, rules or guidelines people set for themselves to determine the kind of behavior and treatment they will accept from others and how they will respond if those rules are violated.

personal shopper, a department store employee who helps customers shop or who chooses and presents items for a customer to select.

personal space, the amount of physical space people need between themselves and others in order to feel at ease. Personal space varies depending on the individual and the circumstances.

personal trainer, someone who is employed to work closely with another to improve physical fitness and athletic performance.

persona non grata, a person who is no longer welcome. From Latin, meaning "an unwelcome person".

person perception, *psych*. the mental processes involved in forming impressions of other people.

persuade, *v*. 1. induce someone to do something. 2 convince.

pet, *n*. 1. a tame animal that is cared for affectionately. 2. a person who is favored and indulged. 3. a thing or idea that is cherished. *v*. 4. gently pat, stroke, or caress an animal or person.

petite amie, *French*. girlfriend.

pet name, an affectionate nickname.

philanderer, *n*. a man who frequently pursues casual sexual relationships.

philia, *n. Ancient Greek*. 1. friendship or affection, often translated as brotherly love. 2. in English, the suffix **-philia** often indicates an extreme or abnormal liking or attraction, as in "necrophilia" (attraction to dead people).

pick a quarrel, intentionally start an argument.

pick on [someone], tease or bully someone.

pick [someone] up, 1. give someone a ride. 2. talk or flirt with someone in order to start a sexual or romantic relationship. 3. collect someone or add someone to a group.

pimp, *n*. someone who manages prostitutes and takes a share of their earnings.

plaintiff, *n*. a party who initiates a lawsuit.

platonic love, a close emotional connection based on a spiritual bond or great admiration, without a sexual component.

platonic marriage, a marriage that does not include sexual relations.

platonic relationship, a non-sexual relationship.

play date, a time arranged by parents for children to play together.

playing house, 1. a childhood pastime in which children play the roles of adults with domestic responsibilities. 2. a somewhat derogatory term for cohabitation.

playmate, *n.* a child who plays with another.

play the field, *idiom.* date many people without any serious attachments.

pleasantry, *n.* 1. a light hearted or insignificant comment. 2. To **exchange pleasantries** is to engage in small talk or banter.

plural marriage. See POLYGAMY.

plus one, the permitted guest of someone invited to an event.

point the finger, *idiom.* accuse or blame someone.

politeness, *n.* good manners; courteous behavior.

polyamory. SEE POLYGAMY.

polygamy, *n.* the practice of having more than one spouse at a time. A person who practices polygamy is a **polygamist. Polygyny** is polygamy in which one man has multiple wives. **Polyandry** is polygamy in which one woman has multiple husbands. Polygamy is sometimes called **plural marriage**; this term seems to refer mostly to polygyny. See BIGAMY, MONOGAMY.

 Group marriage usually refers to an arrangement involving three or more people in a household. In polygyny and polyandry, one person has multiple opposite-sex spouses. In group marriage, there may be multiple males and females, and all the males are considered married to all the females. In some cases, the parties consider themselves all married to each other (although they do not necessarily all engage in sexual relationships with each other). Group marriage is sometimes called **communal marriage**.

 Polyamory is sometimes used as a synonym for group marriage, but more often refers to arrangements where the involved parties do not all consider themselves married and do not necessarily share a household. Polyamory may also refer to **open marriage**, an arrangement in which a socially monogamous couple agrees to be sexually nonmonogamous.

poor relation, *idiom.* 1. someone or something considered inferior to other members of a group. 2. a relative with little money.

pop the question, *idiom.* propose marriage.

popular, *adj.* liked or approved of by people in general.

positional power, authority over others based upon a person's position in an organization.

posse, *n.* 1. a group formed to enforce the law 2. *coll.* an entourage.

possessive, adj. 1. unwilling to share. 2. demanding all of someone's affection and attention. 3. jealously attempting to limit someone's relationships with others.

POSSLQ, *abbr.* persons of the opposite sex sharing living quarters. (Often pronounced POSS-ul-cue.) A term coined in the 1970s by the U.S. Census Bureau in an attempt to determine the prevalence of cohabitation. It was eventually replaced by the classification "unmarried partners".

posthumous marriage, marriage to a dead person. In France, if an engaged person dies, there are some conditions under which the surviving fiancée may receive permission to officially register the marriage as if it had taken place shortly before the death. There are also a few cases in different countries where a governing body permitted posthumous marriage in recognition of special circumstances, and other cases where the families of deceased persons conducted marriage ceremonies on behalf of the dead. See GHOST MARRIAGE.

postnuptial agreement, a written contract signed by spouses during the marriage, often referred to informally as a **postnup**. Typically the purpose is to change or clarify the couple's financial arrangements. Some couples use postnups for non-financial matters, such as allocating housework, or to resolve disagreements. Non-financial provisions are usually not legally binding. Not all legal jurisdictions recognize postnups as valid.

postremogeniture, *n.* a system of inheritance which favors the youngest son. Also called **ultimogeniture**.

power behind the throne, *idiom.* 1. a person or group that controls the one who appears to be in charge. 2. a person who may appear to have no authority, but who has great influence.

praise, *v.* 1. express approval or admiration. *n.* 2. the act of expressing approval or admiration. 3. compliments or words of approval.

pregnancy, *n.* gestation.

premarital, *adj.* before marriage.

premarital counseling, therapy or classes for engaged couples.

prenuptial agreement, a written contract signed by spouses prior to marriage, often referred to informally as a **prenup**. Typically the agreement lists each person's assets and debts, and specifies the distribution of property in the event of divorce or death. Prenups are often used by wealthy people who want to protect family and business interests, people who want to provide for children from prior relationships, people who need to be protected from a spouse's debts, or those who simply want to clarify their financial rights and obligations. Prenups can override some provisions of community property or equitable distribution laws. However, states place limits on what can be legally included in a prenuptial agreement. Some people create prenups with detailed agreements about behavior and lifestyle, but these are usually not legally enforceable. Prenups may also be called premarital agreements, antemarital agreements, and similar terms.

present, *n.* a gift.

primary caregiver, **primary caretaker**, 1. the adult who has the greatest share of responsibility for the care and upbringing of a child. 2. a person in charge of providing care and assistance to a sick, disabled, or elderly person.

primary relative. See RELATIVE.

primogeniture, *n.* a system of inheritance that favors the first-born son.

Prince Charming 1. a standard character in fairy tales; a prince who comes to the rescue of a damsel in distress. 2. an idealized fantasy of one's future husband.

prisoner, *n.* 1. someone legally confined in a jail or prison. 2. someone captured and confined by an enemy or criminal. 3. someone who is or feels restrained by circumstances.

privacy, *n.* 1. the state of being away from public view; freedom from surveillance. 2. freedom from unwanted intrusions. 3. freedom from having personal information disclosed to others.

privacy fence, a fence built to prevent public view or intrusion.

private, *adj.* 1. belonging to or used by a particular individual or group. 2. personal or intimate; not shared with outsiders. 3. secluded; free from interruptions. 4. not available to the general public. 5. not part of government institutions.

procreate, *v.* produce offspring.

projection, *n. psych.* attributing one's own feelings or motives to someone else.

promiscuous, *adj.* 1. having many sexual partners on an informal basis. 2. having an indiscriminate approach.

promise ring, a ring given to a significant other as a symbol of love and loyalty. Promise rings are sometimes used as "pre-engagement" rings by those who intend or hope to become formally engaged at a future date. See ENGAGEMENT RING, FRIENDSHIP RING.

propinquity, *n.* 1. proximity. 2. close kinship. 3. similarity. 4. the state of being close in time.

proposal, *n.* 1. a suggestion or offer. 2. an offer of marriage.

propose, *v.* 1. suggest something to be done or considered. 2. nominate someone for a position. 3. ask someone to marry.

prosocial behavior, a pattern of helpful, caring behavior that benefits others.

prostitute, *n.* a person who engages in sexual relations for money.

protégé (*masc.* or *fem.*), **protégée** (*fem.*), *n.* a person who receives protection and guidance from someone who is interested in his or her career or future prospects.

proud of [someone], *idiom.* feeling pleasure, satisfaction, or admiration for the accomplishments of a family member, friend, associate, or peer.

provider, *n.* someone who provides financial support, especially for a family.

provoke, *v.* 1. make angry 2. stimulate an emotion or reaction. 3. incite an action.

proximity, *n.* the state of being physically close to something or someone.

proximity principle, 1. a principle of social psychology that describes the tendency of people who are near each other to form interpersonal relationships. 2. Gestalt principle of proximity: a tendency for people to perceive objects that are close together as a group.

psychoanalysis, *n. psych.* a method of psychological therapy, originating with Sigmund Freud, which aims to uncover unconscious emotions and motives. A professional who practices psychoanalysis is a **psychoanalyst.**

psychopath, *n.* a sociopath, especially one who is violent.

psychotherapy, *n.* treating emotional or mental problems using psychological techniques, especially interaction with a psychologist or other professional. A professional who practices psychotherapy is a **psychotherapist.**

public servant, a government employee.

pull the wool over [someone]'s eyes, *idiom.* deceive someone.

punching bag, *idiom.* a person who is the habitual victim of a violent abuser. Derived from boxing, where a punching bag is a piece of equipment designed to be repeatedly hit.

punish, *v.* 1. hurt or penalize someone as retribution for an offense. 2. subject a person or group to harsh treatment.

pupil, *n.* a young student.

puppet, *n.* 1. a figure representing a person or creature, manipulated by hand, strings, or rods as play or as a public performance. 2. a person who is controlled by someone else.

puppy love, *idiom.* a temporary crush or infatuation between children.

purse dog, *idiom.* a pet dog small enough to be carried in one's purse.

put [someone] down, i*diom.* make disparaging remarks about someone. (However, to put an animal down is to euthanize it.)

put [someone] in his/her place, *idiom.* demonstrate to someone that he or she is not particularly important, or that he or she has little or no power.

put [someone] on a pedestal, *idiom.* idealize someone.

put [someone] up, 1. provide temporary lodging for someone. 2. propose someone for an appointed or elected position: "We decided to put him up for club president."

put up with, tolerate.

put yourself in someone else's shoes, *idiom.* generate empathy for someone by imagining yourself in that person's situation.

Pyramus and Thisbe, a story by the Roman poet Ovid (43BC-17AD). Two young people fall in love despite their families' enmity, and eventually commit suicide rather than live without each other. The same plot appears in many other stories, notably Shakespeare's *Romeo and Juliet*.

Pygmalion, in mythology, a sculptor who fell in love with a statue he had created, which was then brought to life by the goddess Aphrodite. Pygmalion was the inspiration for a play by George Bernard Shaw, later made into the musical "My Fair Lady". The story is sometimes invoked in reference to someone who tries to remake another person.

quadruplet. See MULTIPLES.

quarrel, *n.* an angry disagreement or argument.

quintuplet. See MULTIPLES.

R

raise a child, take care of a child until maturity.

rank, *n.* 1. a group of people who form a class or level in a hierarchy. 2. a social or official status or position. 3. a position in the armed forces or similar organization. 4. one's status in comparison to others.

rape, *n.* 1. the act of forcing someone to have sexual intercourse. 2. **statutory rape**, sexual intercourse with a person under the age of consent, whether or not force is used. ("Statutory" means that an offense is recognized by written laws -- statutes.)
    The terms **date rape** and **acquaintance rape** are sometimes used to describe rape perpetrated by someone known to the victim. **Marital rape** refers to the rape of one spouse by the other. **Rape by deception** is a crime in which the perpetrator gains the victim's consent through some kind of fraud, such as using a false identity.

rapport, *n.* a harmonious relationship characterized by mutual understanding.

rear, *v. archaic.* take care of children (or animals) until they are grown.

rebound, *v.* 1. bounce back from an impact. 2. recover from an upsetting or traumatic experience. 3. **on the rebound**, having recently experienced rejection or the breakup of a relationship. 4. **rebound relationship**, the first romantic relationship someone has after a rejection or breakup.

rebuff, *v.* 1. abruptly or rudely reject. *n.* 2. the act of rebuffing.

reciprocal, *adj.* felt, given, or done each to the other or in return; mutual.

reciprocity, *n.* the act or practice of mutual exchange.

recluse, *n.* a person who lives in seclusion; one who has a solitary life and avoids other people.

reconcile, *v.* 1. settle a disagreement. 2. restore friendly relations. 3. make disparate ideas compatible.

reconciliation, *n.* 1. the act or state of resuming friendly relations. 2. the act of creating compatibility or consistency.

reindeer games, *idiom.* enjoyable activities which exclude outsiders. From the song "Rudolph the Red-Nosed Reindeer" (1949) by Johnny Marks, based on a character in a children's story (1939) by Robert L. May.

related, *adj.* 1. connected or associated. 2. connected by kinship or marriage.

relation, *n.* 1. a connection or significant association between two or more things or people. 2. a person who is connected by kinship or marriage.

relational transgression, a violation of a rule or agreement (explicit or implicit) in a relationship.

relations, *n.* 1. connections which exist between people or groups. 2. relatives. 3. sexual intercourse.

relationship, *n.* 1. a connection, association, involvement, or correlation between two or more people or things. 2. a connection by blood or marriage. 3. an emotional involvement between people.

relationship coach, a person who encourages and counsels clients on developing the skills needed to improve their personal and business relationships.

relative, *n.* 1. a member of one's extended family. 2. someone who is connected by blood, marriage, or adoption.
   In genetics, **primary relatives** are those with whom one shares approximately half one's genes: parents and siblings. **Secondary relatives** share one-quarter of their genes: grandparents, aunts, uncles. **Tertiary relatives** share one-eighth of their genes: great-grandparents, first cousins.
   Anthropology and sociology sometimes define these relationships differently. **Primary relatives** are one's parents, siblings, spouses, and offspring. **Secondary relatives** are the primary relatives of one's primary relatives, such as one's father's father, mother's brother, and sister's husband. **Tertiary relatives** are the primary relatives of one's secondary relatives, such as one's father's brother's wife.

relict, *n. obs.* a widow.

remarry, *v.* 1. enter into a new marriage after being divorced or widowed. 2. enter into a second (or more) marriage with the same person from whom one was previously divorced.

rendezvous, *n.* an agreed-upon meeting at a specific place and time, usually between two people or two groups.

renter, *n.* a person who uses or occupies property in exchange for payment; a tenant.

reputation, *n.* 1. widespread beliefs or opinions about someone or something. 2. the estimation of a person's character, abilities, and other qualities by the community or the general public.

resent, *v.* feel indignant or bitter over an insult, injury, or unfairness.

resentment, *n.* a feeling of bitterness or anger in response to an insult, injury, or unfairness.

respect, *n.* 1. deep admiration or esteem for a person based on their character, abilities, or other qualities. 2. deference shown to a person based on rank, position, rights, or privileges. *v.* 3. feel or show deference or admiration.

retaliate, *v.* make an insult or injury in response to a similar insult or injury.

reunion, *n.* 1. a meeting or gathering of friends, relatives, or associates after a period of separation. 2. an instance of two or more people coming together after a time apart.

revenge, *n.* punishment or retaliation for wrongs or injuries; vengeance.

right-hand man, **right-hand woman**, *idiom.* an indispensable assistant.

ritual insults, a kind of competition found in many cultures, in which participants demonstrate their verbal skills by insulting each other in clever ways.

rival, *n.* 1. a competitor or opponent. 2. someone who may be perceived as equal or better in a particular activity or endeavor.

rivalry, *n.* a competition; the state of competing with another.

road rage, *idiom.* a disproportionate reaction of extreme anger, and sometimes violence, triggered by irritation or frustration with someone else's driving behavior.

rob the cradle, *idiom.* be involved in a romantic relationship or marriage with someone significantly younger than oneself.

role, *n.* 1. a part played by an actor. 2. a function or pattern of behavior expected of someone based on their position in society or within a group. 3. the function or behavior assumed by someone in a particular situation.

role model, an admired person who is considered an example to be imitated.

role play, role-playing, 1. a game or performance in which participants assume the actions and personalities of persons other than themselves. 2. a psychology technique in which people act out different roles for the purpose of gaining insight or changing behavior.

role reversal, 1. a situation in which two people have exchanged duties and responsibilities, so that each does what the other would normally do. 2. a role playing game or exercise in which two people assume each other's personalities.

romance, *n.* 1. a love relationship. 2. a feeling of excitement and mystery associated with love. 3. a novel or story focusing on love and relationships. 4. a historical narrative depicting heroism, amazing events, and chivalry.

romantic, *adj.* 1. pertaining to love and romance. 2. conducive to or evoking feelings of romance. 3. characterized by an idealized view of love and one's beloved. 4. fanciful, idealistic, or unrealistic. 5. pertaining to a style of literature popular in the early 19th century.

Romeo, *n.* 1. the male protagonist in Shakespeare's play *Romeo and Juliet.* 2. an ardent lover or suitor. 3. a man who pursues romantic relationships with many women.

Romeo and Juliet, a play by William Shakespeare. Two young people fall in love despite their families' enmity, and eventually commit suicide rather than live without each other. Sometimes used to refer to a young couple who are intensely in love, particularly when they appear obsessive or melodramatic.

roomie, *n. inf.* roommate.

roommate, *n.* someone who shares living quarters.

rub [someone] the wrong way, *idiom.* irritate or annoy someone.

rude, *adj.* impolite, especially deliberately so.

ruffle [someone]'s feathers, *idiom.* annoy or irritate someone. Derived from the idea that a bird ruffles its feathers when upset.

rule the roost, *idiom.* be in control of a family or organization.

ruler, *n.* a person who controls or governs; a monarch or sovereign.

running mate, a candidate who joins another to run for related elected positions, such as president and vice-president.

S

Sadie Hawkins Day, a pseudo-holiday taking place in November, inspired by a story line in Al Capp's comic strip, *Li'l Abner* (1934-1978). The fictional holiday encouraged gender role-reversal, with women asking men on dates or proposing marriage. See LEAP DAY.

Saint Valentine's Day. See VALENTINE'S DAY.

same-sex marriage or **gay marriage**, a marriage between persons of the same sex.

sandwich generation, *idiom*. people in midlife who have the responsibility of caring for aging parents while still supporting dependent children.

scapegoat, *n*. someone who is made to take the blame for others or suffer in their place. In ancient times, a scapegoat was a goat released into the wilderness to symbolically carry away the sins of the people.

schoolmate, *n*. a classmate or fellow student.

scion, *n*. a descendant, especially of a wealthy or socially prominent family.

séance, seance, *n*. a meeting at which people attempt to contact the dead. A person who conducts a séance and claims to communicate with the dead is called a **medium.**

second banana, *idiom*. 1. a performer in a comedy act whose role is to support the lead performer. 2. anyone serving in a secondary role.

secretary, *n*. 1. a person employed to handle correspondence and perform routine business functions in an office. 2. an official who is in charge of the records of an organization. 3. an official who is in charge of managing a government department.

secondary relative. SEE RELATIVE.

secret, *n*. 1. something that is hidden or unknown to others. *adj*. 2. unseen or unknown to others.

secretive, *adj.* tending to keep information, feelings, or intentions hidden.

seduce, *v.* 1. lead astray; lure someone away from duty or proper conduct. 2. entice someone into sexual activity. 3. lure or entice.

seduction, *n.* 1. the act of seducing or being seduced. 2. *obs.* historically, the crime of using trickery, especially a promise of marriage, to persuade a woman to engage in sexual activity.

see eye to eye, *idiom.* agree.

self-concept, *n.* the beliefs, thoughts, and perceptions one has about oneself.

self-esteem, *n.* 1. a favorable opinion of oneself. 2. a person's overall evaluation of his or her own value.

selfish, *adj.* overly concerned with one's own advantages and enjoyments with little or no concern for others.

self-worth, *n.* self-esteem.

send [someone] packing, *idiom.* require someone to leave a home, job, or location.

senior, *n.* 1. a person who is older than another. 2. a person past midlife, also called a **senior citizen.** 3. a person in the final year of high school or college. *adj.* 4. older than someone else. 5. having higher or the highest rank or professional standing.

separated, *adj.* referring to marital status: living apart from one's spouse.

separation, *n.* 1. the state of living apart after having been married or cohabiting. 2. the state of being at a distance from a spouse, close friend, or family member. See TRIAL SEPARATION.

seraglio. See HAREM.

serf, *n.* historically, a peasant in bondage to a lord or wealthy landowner, required to live and work on the land in exchange for protection.

serial monogamy. See MONOGAMY.

servant, *n.* a person employed to perform domestic duties.

service animal, a specially trained animal (such as a guide dog) that assists people with disabilities. See THERAPY ANIMAL.

settle, *v.* 1. in reference to a dispute or lawsuit: to come to an agreement or resolution. 2. *coll.* in reference to marriage: to pragmatically accept a partner whom one considers less than ideal.

settle down, 1. establish a steady routine or secure way of life, especially one that includes marriage. 2. become calm. 3. become focused on a task.

set one's cap for [someone], *idiom.* attempt to attract a particular suitor. From the 18th century, when women always wore some kind of head covering, based on the idea of putting on one's very best cap in order to appear attractive.

set up, *v. idiom.* introduce two people with the hope that they will be attracted to each other.

setup, *n. idiom.* a meeting between two people arranged by a friend with the hope that they will be attracted to each other.

seven year itch, *idiom.* the belief that married couples begin to lose interest in each other at around the seventh anniversary. There is no scientific evidence to support seven years as more or less significant than any other time period. The phrase originated in the 1800s as the name of an itchy skin infection thought to last seven years.

sex, *n.* 1. the classification of being either female or male. 2. males or females collectively. 3. the sum of all the physical differences between males and females, or the phenomena and behavior dependent on those differences. 4. sexual intercourse.

sex role, a set of behaviors considered acceptable and appropriate for one's sex within a particular culture or society.

sext, *v. slang.* send sexually-oriented text messages.

sexual intercourse, genital contact, especially insertion of the penis into the vagina.

share, *v.* 1. distribute portions of something. 2. jointly use or participate. 3. reveal personal information or ideas to others. *n.* 4. a portion or allotment of something to be received or contributed. 5. **fair share**, the quantity or size of a portion or allotment one reasonably expects to receive.

ships that pass in the night, *idiom*. people who encounter each other only once. From a poem by Henry Wadsworth Longfellow.

shoot the breeze, *idiom*. have a casual conversation.

shotgun wedding, *idiom*. a wedding precipitated by pregnancy or to avoid sexual scandal. The expression is based on a hypothetical scenario in which the couple is forced to get married by the bride's angry, shotgun-wielding father.

shoulder to cry on, *idiom*. someone who is available to listen to one's problems and to provide sympathy.

shower, *n*. a party given to celebrate an upcoming wedding or the imminent arrival of a baby, by "showering" the guest of honor with gifts.

shun, *v*. avoid or ostracize someone.

Siamese twins. See CONJOINED TWINS.

sibling, *n*. a brother or sister. All the children of the same two parents are siblings to each other. Half siblings have only one parent in common.

sibling rivalry, competition or animosity between siblings.

side of the family, the relatives of one parent or the other.

sidekick, *n*. a companion or assistant.

significant other, 1. a person with whom one has an established romantic or sexual relationship. 2. a friend or family member who provides support and companionship.

silence means/implies consent, *proverb*. failure to disagree is tacit agreement.

silent partner, a business partner who does not participate actively in the business.

silver anniversary or **silver wedding**, a couple's 25th wedding anniversary.

single, *adj.* 1. not married. Traditionally, this describes someone who has never been married, in contrast to being divorced or widowed, but it is often used broadly to mean anyone who is not currently married or cohabiting. Some people extend the meaning further to mean they are not dating someone steadily.

singles, *pl. n.* people who are not married.

singles bar, a bar whose customers are primarily unmarried people hoping to meet others.

singleton, *n.* a baby born singly (as differentiated from MULTIPLES).

sing [someone]'s praises, *idiom.* enthusiastically and publicly praise someone.

sister, *n.* 1. a female sibling. 2. a very close female friend, treated like a sister. 3. a nun or member of a religious order. 4. a female member of the same church. 5. a fellow member of an association, such as a sorority. 6. a thing that is regarded as having kinship with a similar thing, such as sister cities.

sisterhood, *n.* 1. the condition of being a sister; the relationship between sisters. 2. a feeling of close friendship. 3. an organization of women, such as a sorority. 4. women who share similar qualities and interests.

sister-in-law, *pl.* sisters-in-law. *n.* the wife of one's brother or the sister of one's husband.

sister-wife, *n.* 1. a woman who is married to her brother or half-brother. 2. a woman who is married, polygamously, to the same husband as her sister. 3. a co-wife in a polygamous marriage.

sitter, *n.* babysitter.

slander, *n.* 1. malicious, false statements about someone. *v.* 2. utter malicious, false statements.

slave, *n.* a person who is subjected to involuntary servitude; someone who is treated like property.

slavery, *n.* 1. the condition of being a slave. 2. the practice of owning or trading in slaves. Selling and transporting slaves is also known as

human trafficking. Although slavery is now illegal everywhere in the world, it is still common.

sleepover, *n*. an occasion of spending the night away from home, especially as part of a children's activity.

slumber party, a party for children or teenagers at which they spend the night at the host's home.

small talk, polite conversation about unimportant matters.

smitten, *adj*. 1. very much in love, especially at first sight; infatuated.

smooch, *v.* or *n*. kiss.

snake in the grass, *idiom*. a treacherous person.

snitch, *v. slang*. 1. inform on someone. *n*. 2. an informer.

snob, *n*. 1. one who believes oneself to have superior social rank, intellectual superiority, more highly cultivated taste, etc., and behaves condescendingly toward others. 2. one who believes oneself to be an expert in a field and is condescending toward those with different tastes or opinions. 3. one who obsessively seeks out, imitates, and prefers those of high social rank.

snub, *v*. 1. rebuff or ignore someone. *n*. 2. an act or incident of snubbing.

snuggle, *v*. cuddle.

SO, *abbr*. significant other.

sociable, *adj*. friendly in the company of others.

sociability, *n*. 1. the quality of being sociable. 2. the ability to get along with others.

social butterfly, *idiom*, a person (usually female) who is happy in social situations and who tries to spend some time talking with many people and moving among various groups at an event.

social circle, See CIRCLE.

social climber, someone who tries to move into a group with higher social status.

social contract, the theory that people voluntarily surrender some of their freedom in order to cooperate with others and thus obtain the benefits of an orderly society.

social disease, *obs.* a sexually transmitted disease. See STD.

social exchange theory, *psych.* a theory that proposes that social behavior is based on a process intended to maximize the benefits and minimize the costs of involvement in relationships. This is sometimes called the **minimax principle**.

social facilitation, *psych.* the tendency of people to perform differently on tasks when others are present. See COACTION EFFECT and AUDIENCE EFFECT.

social identity, 1. that part of a person's self-concept that is derived from membership and status in a group. 2. the way one is perceived by others based on one's role and status within a group.

social identity theory, *psych.* a theory developed by Henri Tajfel and John Turner that describes and predicts social behavior, based on the ways in which people identify themselves as part of a group and their perceptions of differences in status between groups.

social integration, *soc.* the extent to which an individual feels connected to a community or group.

socialize, *v.* 1. associate or mingle with others. 2. teach someone to behave in a socially acceptable way.

social media, websites and applications that provide forums or online communities for activities such as blogging, sharing information and pictures, and sending messages.

social network, an interconnected group of people.

social networking, the use of websites and applications to interact with others.

Social Register, a book listing information about individuals and families considered socially elite by the book's publishers.

social role, *soc.* a set of expected behaviors and norms based on one's position in society.

social skills, the skills needed to successfully communicate and interact with others.

social worker, a person whose job is to provide assistance to individuals, families and children who face problems in their everyday lives. A **clinical social worker** or **psychiatric social worker** also diagnoses and treats emotional, mental, and behavioral problems. Social workers are typically employed by government agencies, health care facilities, and nonprofit organizations.

society, *n.* 1. a group of people organized for a specific purpose. 2. people in general, viewed as a community. 3. an organized system that provides a structure for the security and identity of a large community of people.

sociopath, *n.* someone with the traits of antisocial personality disorder.

son, *n.* 1. one's male child. 2. a male descendant.

son-in-law, *pl.* sons-in-law. *n.* the husband of one's child.

sororate marriage, a practice in which a man marries his wife's sister, typically after the death of the first wife, but sometimes polygamously. In some cultures this type of marriage has been encouraged as a way of maintaining family alliances, while in others it is forbidden. See LEVIRATE MARRIAGE.

sorority, *n.* an organization of female students.

soulmate, *n.* 1. a person with whom one has an especially strong affinity, especially a romantic partner. 2. a person one feels predestined to meet.

sounding board, a person or group whose reactions to an idea or proposal serve as a measure of its potential acceptability, popularity or effectiveness.

space. See INVADE SOMEONE'S SPACE, MORE SPACE, PERSONAL SPACE.

spark, *n.* a feeling of attraction or interest.

spat, *n.* a petty disagreement.

speak the same language, *idiom.* be in agreement.

speech accommodation, *ling.* the theory that people in conversations adjust their speech patterns in response to the speech patterns of others.

speech community, *ling.* a group of people who share a language and dialect, and who also share a set of norms and expectations about the use of language.

speed dating, a social activity in which people seeking romantic relationships have a series of brief conversations with potential partners to determine whether there is mutual interest.

sperm donor, 1. a man who donates sperm, usually anonymously, to a fertility clinic or sperm bank. 2. sometimes used derogatively to refer to a father who has abused, neglected, or abandoned his children. See BIRTH FATHER.

spinster, *n. archaic.* a woman who has remained unmarried beyond the usual age for marriage. Now considered derogatory. Historically, the word meant one who spins (makes thread or yarn), an occupation typically done by females.

spite, *n.* 1. a malicious desire to harm or annoy someone. 2. an action taken for the sole purpose of harming or annoying someone. *v.* 3. perform an action for the purpose of annoying or harming another.

spite fence, a fence built solely for the purpose of annoying or inconveniencing a neighbor.

spiteful, *adj.* malicious.

split up, *v.* 1. separate or end a relationship. 2. physically separate two or more people.

spokesman, spokeswoman, spokesperson, *n.* a person who is designated to speak on behalf of someone else or for an organization.

sponsor, *n.* 1. someone who vouches for another or is responsible for another. 2. a person who assumes responsibility for an infant at baptism. 3. someone who provides guidance or mentoring during a period of instruction or probation.

spoon, *v.* 1. lie with a partner, one behind the other, so the bodies are nestled together like spoons. 2. *archaic.* show romantic affection.

sports widow, *idiom*. a person, usually a woman, who is left alone for long periods of time while her partner watches or engages in a favorite sport. The phrase is often adapted for particular sports or other activities: football widow, computer widow, etc.

spousal maintenance, **spousal support**. See ALIMONY.

spouse, *n*. a married person.

spurn, *v*. reject with contempt.

squabble. *n*. a petty argument.

squad, *n*. 1. a small group of soldiers or police officers. 2. a small group of people engaged in a common task. 3. a small team of sports players.

stalk, *v*. 1. approach or pursue prey in a stealthy manner. 2. walk in a stiff or angry manner. 3. obsessively harass, terrorize, or spy on someone.

stalker *n*. 1. someone who stalks. 2. a prowler or someone who sneaks about, typically with unlawful intentions. 3. a person who harasses or terrorizes another by obsessively following, spying, engaging in unwanted contact, intimidating, causing trouble, or threatening. This kind of stalking is now illegal in most states.

stand [someone] up, *idiom*. fail to show up for a date or other appointment with someone. To be **stood up** is to wait for someone who doesn't arrive.

stand up to [someone], *idiom*. confront or oppose someone, especially when refusing to accept unfair or abusive treatment.

Stanford Prison Experiment, a psychological experiment conducted in 1971 at Stanford University. Volunteers were assigned roles of prisoners and guards, and placed in a simulated prison environment. The experimenters ended the study prematurely because of the escalation of brutality and other behavioral problems.

star-crossed lovers, lovers whose relationship is doomed to fail. From Shakespeare's *Romeo and Juliet*.

stare [someone] down, *idiom*. look directly at someone, especially in a confrontational manner, until he or she feels compelled to look away or leave.

staring contest, a game in which two people stare into each other's eyes until one of them cannot resist blinking or looking away.

starter marriage, *idiom.* a first marriage that lasts only a few years. Typically used facetiously or derogatively.

statutory rape. See RAPE.

STD, *abbr.* sexual transmitted disease. A disease that is transmitted solely or primarily through sexual contact. Also called **STI,** sexually transmitted infection.

step-, a prefix indicating a family connection formed by remarriage, not by blood. For example, a **stepmother** is a woman who occupies the position of mother by marriage to one's father. A **stepbrother** or **stepsister** is one's stepparent's child from a previous relationship.

stepfamily. See FAMILY.

step on [someone]'s toes, *idiom.* upset someone by interfering with responsibilities or rights.

steward, *n.* 1. someone who manages another's property or finances. 2. someone who is employed to be in charge of a household. 3. someone who is in charge of tables, wine, or other matters at a restaurant. 4. someone on a vessel, airplane, or train who is in charge of the comfort of passengers. 5. **stewardess,** *archaic.* a female flight attendant.

Stockholm syndrome, a psychological phenomenon in which hostages develop sympathetic feelings for their captors and may identify with or defend them. Named after an occurrence in 1973 in which hostages held for six days following a bank robbery in Stockholm became emotionally attached to their captors.

stonewall, *v.* 1. delay or block someone's requests or questions by refusing to answer or giving evasive replies. 2. obstruct someone's progress. 3. emotionally withdraw from personal interaction, typically by minimizing or refusing verbal responses and failing to respond nonverbally.

stood up. See STAND SOMEONE UP.

stool pigeon, stoolie, *idiom.* a police informant, especially someone who informs on his criminal associates.

straight man, an entertainer who plays the role of foil for a comedian.

strange bedfellows, *idiom.* seemingly mismatched people who have formed unlikely alliances. Often used in a political context.

stranger, *n.* 1. an unknown person. 2. a newcomer or outsider. 3. someone who is unacquainted with something.

student, *n.* 1. someone enrolled in school. 2. someone who is engaged in learning.

subordinate, *n.* someone of lower rank.

succubus, *n.* a demon or evil spirit believed to appear in female form and engage in sexual intercourse with men as they sleep. See INCUBUS.

sugar daddy, *idiom.* a wealthy man who provides gifts and financial support to a younger woman in exchange for a sexual relationship.

suitor, *n.* a man who pursues a relationship with marriage in mind.

superior, *n.* 1. someone of a higher rank. 2. someone who is better than another in skill, talent, or character. *adj.* 3. better.

supervisor, *n.* 1. someone who directs or trains workers. 2. someone who is in charge of a project or business.

surname, *n.* a family name, as distinguished from a person's given name. Also called **last name** because, in English, it is generally written or spoken after the given name; however, in many cultures the surname comes first.

surrogate, *n.* a substitute; someone appointed to act for another.

surrogate father, someone who takes on the role of a father.

surrogate mother, 1. someone who takes on the role of a mother. 2. someone who bears a child on behalf of a woman unable to bear a child. A **traditional surrogate** is artificially inseminated with the father's sperm. She is the child's biological mother because it is her egg that is fertilized. A **gestational surrogate** is implanted with an embryo conceived using the mother's egg and the father's sperm (or, in some cases, a donor egg and/or donor sperm). She is not the biological mother, because her egg is not used, but she is the birth mother, because she carries and gives birth to the child.

suspect, *v.* 1. have the impression that something is true without complete proof: "I suspect that he lied on his job application" 2. have an impression that someone is guilty or dishonest. 3. have an impression that something is hidden or that things are not as they seem. *n.* 4. a person who is thought to have committed a crime or misdeed.

suspicion, *n.* 1. a feeling of distrust or a sense that something is wrong. 2. a thought or feeling that something is likely: "She had a suspicion that that the computer was infected." 3. the state of being distrusted or thought guilty: "The police considered him under suspicion for several crimes."

suspicious, *adj.* 1. having a feeling of distrust or a sense that something is wrong or that things are not as they appear to be. 2. behaving or appearing in a way that causes others to feel suspicion.

sweetheart, *n.* 1. one's lover or darling. 2. an endearment.

sweet on [someone], *idiom.* having a crush on someone.

swept off one's feet, *idiom.* overwhelmed romantically.

swinging, *n. idiom.* a lifestyle in which socially monogamous couples agree to engage in outside sexual relationships. The outside relationships are generally of short duration and usually do not include romantic attachment. Swinging is sometimes referred to as **open marriage** or **wife swapping**. See POLYGAMY.

sycophant, *n.* a servile flatterer; one who behaves obsequiously and praises influential people in order to gain personal advantages.

symbiotic relationship, *n.* 1. in biology, a close association between two dissimilar organisms that live together. 2. a relationship between two people in which each contributes something different so that both benefit. 3. a relationship in which two people are mutually dependent; it may or may not be beneficial to both parties.

sympathy, *n.* 1. a feeling of compassion. 2. harmony or agreement of feelings between people.

take a fancy to [someone], *idiom.* develop a strong interest or affection for someone.

take after [someone], *idiom.* resemble a parent or other family member. (However, to **take off after** someone is to follow or chase someone.)

take [someone/something] for granted, *idiom.* 1. automatically assume that something is true. 2. fail to appreciate the value of someone or something.

take [someone] to wife, *archaic.* marry a woman.

take [someone] under one's wing, *idiom.* provide protective assistance or guidance for someone. From the concept of a mother bird protecting her chicks under her wing.

take to [someone], *idiom.* like someone.

talk back to, reply in a rude or defiant manner.

talk turkey, *idiom.* talk seriously and pragmatically.

tattle, *v.* 1. reveal another's improper activities or secrets. 2. gossip.

tattletale, *n.* someone who reveals others' secrets, especially a child who reports the misdeeds of other children to teachers or parents.

teach, *v.* 1. explain or show someone how to do something; give instructions. 2. impart knowledge or information.

teacher, *n.* someone who teaches; an instructor.

teacher's pet, a student who receives preferential treatment from a teacher.

team, *n.* a group of people associated in a sport or joint endeavor.

teammate, *n.* a person who is on the same team.

tease, *v*. 1. persistently provoke, irritate or taunt a person or animal, either playfully or cruelly. 2. deliberately tantalize a person or animal. *n*. 3. a person or action that attempts to provoke attention and interest by tantalizing.

tell [someone] off, *idiom*. angrily rebuke someone.

tenant, *n*. a person who occupies or uses land or buildings owned by someone else, usually for rent.

tertiary relative. See RELATIVE.

tête-a-tête, an intimate conversation between two people. French, meaning "head to head".

text, *v*. 1. send short messages between mobile devices via SMS (short message service). *n*. 2. a short message sent or received on a mobile device. 3. the main body of a written or published work. 4. the original words of an author or speaker.

Thelma and Louise, the title characters in a 1991 film written by Callie Khouri and directed by Ridley Scott. Two friends set off for a weekend road trip and end up running from the law. Sometimes used to refer to a pair of great female friends who have adventures together.

therapy animal, a specially trained animal (typically a dog) that provides comfort and affection to people in hospitals, nursing homes, and other institutions, to people in disaster areas, or to those with learning difficulties. Sometimes called a **comfort animal**. See SERVICE ANIMAL.

thick as thieves, *idiom*. having a very close friendship; sharing secrets.

third party, a person or group that is only incidentally involved in an agreement, dispute, or interaction between two parties.

thrall, *n*. 1. the condition of being in someone's power, especially as a result of psychological manipulation. 2. *archaic*. a slave or captive.

three musketeers, a group of three very close or inseparable friends. From the title characters of the 1844 novel by Alexandre Dumas.

threesome, *n*. a group of three.

through thick and thin, *idiom*. through both good and bad times.

throw [someone] to the wolves, *idiom.* 1. abandon someone facing an ordeal. 2. sacrifice someone for one's own protection. Possibly based on Russian folk tales about parents who abandoned their children to pursuing wolves in order to save the rest of the family.

throw [someone] under the bus, *idiom.* selfishly sacrifice a friend or ally in order to protect oneself.

tie that binds, ties that bind, *idiom.* 1. shared beliefs or experiences that create a bond between people. 2. family relationships that create unity or obligation. Popularized by the 18th century hymn, "Blest Be the Tie That Binds," by John Fawcett.

tie the knot, *idiom.* get married.

tied to [someone]'s apron strings, *idiom.* controlled by someone else, usually one's mother or wife. See MAMA'S BOY.

tiff, *n.* a minor or petty quarrel.

time twins, two unrelated people who happened to be born within a few minutes of each other.

toady, *n.* an obsequious sycophant.

top banana, *idiom.* 1. the leading performer in a comedy act. 2. the leader or boss.

top dog, *idiom.* a victor or leader who has acquired the highest position.

traitor, *n.* 1. someone who betrays a trust. 2. someone who commits treason.

transference, *n. psych.* an unconscious process whereby a psychotherapy client attributes feelings, attitudes, and behaviors of significant people from the past to someone in the present, such as the therapist or a significant other. **Countertransference** is a process in which the therapist has an emotional reaction to the client.

traumatic bonding, trauma bonding, *psych.* a theory describing the development of strong emotional connections between a victim of abuse and the abuser.

trespass, *n.* 1. unauthorized entry on someone else's land or property. 2. a wrongful act that causes injury to someone, their property, or their rights. *v.* 3. wrongfully enter someone else's land. 4. commit a wrongful act against someone.

triad, *n.* a group of three.

trial marriage. See COHABITATION.

trial separation, 1. an arrangement whereby a married couple lives apart to determine whether they want to divorce. 2. a period during which a couple temporarily separates while attempting to resolve problems in the relationship. See SEPARATION.

tribe, *n.* 1. a community of people united by common descent, a history of group traditions, or allegiance to the same leaders. 2. a local division of aboriginal or native people. 3. the children of a very large family.

trigamy, *n.* a facetious term for the act of committing a second bigamy; marrying a third person while still formally married to two previous spouses. A person who commits trigamy is a **trigamist.** See BIGAMY, POLYGAMY.

triplet. See MULTIPLES.

true blue, *idiom.* loyal.

true love's kiss, an element in some fairy tales, in which a person (usually a woman) is rescued from a malady or spell by the kiss of a soulmate or future spouse. Often used as a symbol for love at first sight, falling in love, or fulfilling one's romantic destiny.

trust, *n.* 1. reliance upon the integrity or ability of a person or thing. 2. confidence. 3. responsibility for the safekeeping of valuables. 4. a financial arrangement that allows a third party (trustee) to hold or manage money and property on behalf of beneficiaries or for a specified purpose. *v.* 5. rely upon, or have confidence in, someone or something.

trustee, *n.* someone who has a legal responsibility to manage assets on behalf of another, or for a specified purpose.

trusty, *adj.* 1. reliable. *n.* 2. a well-behaved prisoner who is given special responsibilities and privileges.

trophy wife, *idiom.* a young, attractive wife who functions as a status symbol for an older, wealthy man.

tryst, *n.* a romantic rendezvous.

turn, *n.* an opportunity to act or speak which comes in order or rotation to each individual within a group.

To **take turns** is to do something alternately or in succession. To be **out of turn** is to do something at the wrong time.

turn against, become opposed to someone, or cause others to oppose someone.

turn on [someone], suddenly become hostile toward someone.

turn-taking, *ling.* a formal or informal process by which speakers in a conversation determine who will speak next.

turn the tables, *idiom.* cause a situation between people or groups to be reversed, especially to one's own advantage.

tutor, *n.* 1. someone hired to provide private instruction in a particular subject. 2. a teacher who helps students prepare for examinations. *v.* 3. act as a tutor or private teacher.

T-V distinction, **tu-vous distinction**, *ling.* a system of second-person pronouns, such as the French *tu* and *vous*, where *tu* is a familiar or informal form of address and *vous* is formal or polite. Many languages have similar distinctions, and the social customs for choosing the correct pronoun in a particular relationship vary among cultures.

twin, *n.* 1. one of two children born together. **Identical twins** are the result of a single fertilized egg that splits to form two embryos. **Fraternal twins** occur when two fertilized eggs are implanted in the uterus at the same time. See MULTIPLES. 2. *coll.* one of two people who closely resemble each other.

two's company, three's a crowd, *proverb.* A couple would rather spend time with each other without the presence of a third person.

twosome, *n.* a duo or couple.

two-time, *v.* 1. be unfaithful to a spouse or lover. 2. double cross someone. *adj.* 3. having done something twice.

type, *n.* in the context of dating and relationships: the collection of characteristics and qualities that someone habitually prefers or is attracted to in a partner: "She ignored him because he wasn't her type."

ugly duckling, *idiom.* someone who is perceived as unattractive or lacking in ability, but who eventually becomes beautiful or successful. Based on a story by Hans Christian Anderson, in which a swan hatchling is mistaken for a baby duck.

ultimogeniture. See POSTREMOGENITURE.

unattached, *adj.* single; not involved in a romantic relationship.

uncle, *n.* 1. the brother of one's father or mother. 2. the husband of one's aunt. 3. an honorary title sometimes used by children for men who are family friends.

unconditional love, affection with no limits or conditions; love that is given freely without any restrictions or requirements.

unconditional positive regard, *psych.* in a therapeutic context, accepting the client in a supportive, nonjudgmental manner, regardless of what the person discloses.

uncontested divorce. See CONTESTED DIVORCE.

underage, *adj.* 1. not old enough for a particular privilege or right, such as driving or voting. 2. below the age of consent.

underling, *n.* a subordinate.

under [someone]'s thumb, *idiom.* completely dominated by someone.

unfriend, *v. slang.* remove someone from one's list of contacts on a social networking site.

unrequited, *adj.* when referring to an emotion, especially love: unreturned or unacknowledged.

untouchable, *n.* 1. in India, a member of a low caste whose touch or proximity is thought to defile anyone of a higher caste. Although untouchability was legally banned in 1950, discrimination and human rights abuses against so-called untouchables continue in the 21st century. *adj.* 2. immune to criticism, investigation, or legal action, due to a privileged or protected position. 3. out of reach; unable to be touched.

unwed, *adj.* not married.

uxorial, *adj.* pertaining to a wife.

uxorious, *adj.* excessively affectionate and fond of one's wife.

valentine, *n*. 1. a card or gift presented on Valentine's Day. 2. a person with whom one exchanges affectionate greetings or romantic attention on Valentine's Day.

Valentine's Day, a holiday in honor of romantic love, celebrated every February 14. According to legend, the day is associated with St. Valentine, a Christian priest executed by the Roman emperor Claudius.

valet, *n*. a male servant or employee who takes care of grooming and clothing needs.

vendetta, *n*. 1. a feud undertaken by a murder victim's family for the purpose of getting revenge. 2. a long and vicious feud.

venereal disease, *archaic*. a sexually transmitted disease. See STD.

vengeance, *n*. 1. revenge. 2. **with a vengeance**, to an extreme degree.

verbal duel, a debate or argument, especially one that is formally arranged or intended to display the participants' language skills. See RITUAL INSULTS.

victim, *n*. a person who has been injured, harmed, cheated, or deceived.

virgin, *n*. 1. a person who has never engaged in sexual intercourse. 2. *coll.* a person engaging in an activity for the first time.

visitation rights, the legal rights to spend time with one's children, granted by a court to a noncustodial parent. Visitation rights are sometimes granted to grandparents or other relatives.

vulnerable, *adj*. 1. capable of being physically or emotionally wounded. 2. open to attack or criticism. 3. emotionally open and willing to risk being hurt.

W

waiter (*masc.*), **waitress** (*fem.*), *n.* a person who serves at dining tables, as in a restaurant; a person who serves food and drinks. **Wait staff** or **waitstaff** is a collective noun for all the servers working at a particular location.

walk a mile in [someone]'s shoes, *idiom.* generate empathy for someone by undergoing similar experiences or by imagining oneself in the other's situation.

walk down the aisle, *idiom.* get married. In a traditional ceremony, the newly married couple exits by way of the center aisle.

walk in on [someone], *idiom.* unexpectedly enter a place where someone is engaged in a private or secret activity.

walk out on [someone/something], *idiom.* abandon.

war bride, a woman who marries a soldier during a time of war, especially if he is from another country and she subsequently moves to his country.

ward, *n.* a person who is legally under the care of a guardian or court.

warden, *n.* 1. the chief administrative officer of a prison. 2. a person charged with the care and safekeeping of people, animals, or objects.

watch out for [someone], 1. behave protectively toward someone. 2. be on guard against someone.

wear one's heart on one's sleeve, *idiom.* show one's emotions openly. Possibly derived from the custom in the Middle Ages whereby a knight in a tournament wore a lady's token of affection (such as a handkerchief) pinned to his sleeve.

wear the pants in the house, *idiom.* be the main authority in a household. The expression dates from a historical period when only men were supposed to wear pants (women wore skirts), and equates authority with masculine roles.

wed, *v.* formally marry.

wedded, *adj.* married.

wedding, *n.* 1. a ceremony in which people are united in marriage. A **civil ceremony** is a non-religious legal marriage ceremony performed by a government official or other authorized officiant. A **religious ceremony** is usually performed by a clergyperson. To be legally binding, a marriage must be registered according to the laws of the jurisdiction where it takes place. 2. the anniversary of a wedding.

wedding band, a wedding ring, usually in a simple style.

wedding crasher, an intrusive person who attends a wedding without an invitation. See PARTY CRASHER.

wedding etiquette, ceremonial traditions and rules of behavior practiced at weddings.

wedding march, a musical composition played at a wedding, either at the bride's entrance or at the couple's exit.

wedding night, the first night after a wedding. Often used as a way of referring indirectly to consummation.

wedding planner, a professional employed to oversee the arrangements for a wedding.

wedding ring, a ring, usually made of precious metal such as gold, which is given to one's spouse during the wedding ceremony as a symbol of commitment. Different cultures and religions have different traditions and customs surrounding wedding rings. Wedding rings are usually worn on the third finger (ring finger). Whether they are worn on the left or right hand depends on one's cultural or religious tradition. See ENGAGEMENT RING.

wedding trip. See HONEYMOON.

wedding vows, promises made by the spouses during a wedding ceremony.

wedlock, *n.* marriage.

wet nurse, a woman who is hired to breastfeed another's infant.

whipping boy, *idiom.* someone who is blamed or punished for another's misdeeds. Historically, the sons of royal families often had companions who accepted the whipping or other punishment for any misbehavior of the young prince.

whirlwind romance, *idiom*. a romantic relationship that progresses very quickly.

white lie, a lie that is considered trivial and harmless, especially one intended to avoid hurt feelings or embarrassment.

white wedding, 1. a formal wedding with a traditional ceremony, in which the bride wears a white dress. 2. *archaic*. the wedding of a virgin.

widow (*fem.*) or **widower** (*masc.*), *n*. a person whose spouse has died.

widow's walk, a platform or walkway on the roof of a house, used to watch for incoming ships; so named because of its use by sailors' wives hoping for the return of their husbands.

wife, *pl*. wives. *n*. a married woman.

wife swapping. See SWINGING.

wind/ twist [someone] around one's finger, *idiom*. manipulate and control someone.

wingman, *n. idiom*. a friend who provides guidance and support to another in social situations, especially when trying to meet potential romantic partners. Borrowed from air force terminology: a pilot who provides protective support by flying just outside and behind the right wing of a flight formation's leader.

wink, *v*. briefly blink one eye, typically as a signal to someone.

wolf in sheep's clothing, *idiom*. a treacherous person who pretends to be harmless. From the Bible, in a sermon in the book of Matthew.

womanizer, *n*. philanderer.

woo, *v*. 1. seek someone's love and affection, especially with marriage in mind. 2. attempt to persuade a person or group to do something.

working relationship, the interaction and cooperation needed between colleagues, bosses, and employees. A **good working relationship** is one in which people are on good terms and work well together.

worship the ground [someone] walks on, *idiom.* have deep, uncritical admiration of someone.

xenophobia, *n.* an unreasonable fear or hatred of strangers or foreigners, or of things that are strange or foreign.

yes-man, *n. idiom.* a person who unconditionally agrees with everything said by a boss or associate; a sycophant.

young, *n.* when used as a collective noun: 1. young offspring. 2. young people in general.

Z

zelophobia, *n.* an extreme fear of jealousy.

www.ingramcontent.com/pod-product-compliance
Lightning Source LLC
Chambersburg PA
CBHW071405280526
45787CB00001B/436